The Evangelical Renaissance

Other Books by Donald G. Bloesch

The Evangelical Renaissance

by

DONALD G. BLOESCH

WILLIAM B. EERDMANS PUBLISHING COMPANY
Grand Rapids, Michigan

Copyright © 1973 by William B. Eerdmans Publishing Company
All rights reserved
Library of Congress Catalog Card Number 72-96407
ISBN 0-8028-1527-8
Printed in the United States of America

To
DR. JOHN A. MACKAY

for his loyalty to the faith
once delivered to the saints

Preface

Because I see in the resurgence of evangelicalism today both opportunities and pitfalls, I have been moved to share some thoughts on a direction for evangelical renewal in the future. An analysis has been made of the rise of the new evangelical theology and of the hallmarks of evangelicalism. I have also sought to reassess the contribution of Karl Barth, showing how it is possible to learn from his theology even while not embracing it as the answer for our times. In addition I have seen the need for dispelling the bogey of Pietism, since both ecumenists and evangelicals today should acknowledge their indebtedness to that great spiritual movement in the past which was responsible for the missionary upsurge and the outpouring of charitable enterprises in Protestantism. It can also be shown that a sizable number of Pietists and a great many of the Christian mystics were actively engaged in social and political action. They not only brought revival to the church but helped to turn the destinies of entire nations.

Evangelicals today need to be reminded that biblical religion is not the same as bourgeois religiosity. The true church will forever stand against the stream of the culture, and it will make this stand known in its prophetic criticism. Religion must be united with ethics if it is to have lasting power. The question "What must I do to be saved?" must always be followed by "What ought I to do now that I am saved?"

Those who espouse an evangelical position should not isolate themselves from other Christians if they are to be a bona fide source of renewal for the church today. We must let ourselves be corrected by our Catholic and Orthodox brethren, especially where this is warranted by Scripture. We have much to learn even from liberal Protestants, who have not been entirely off the mark in some of their protests and concerns. The new Social Gospel movement undoubtedly errs in confusing a just society instituted by social engineering with the kingdom of God, but it bids us to recall that there are definite social implications in the biblical message. Evangelicals and liberals can only be reconciled through a common rededication to the message and imperatives of Holy Scripture, and remote though the possibility may seem we should certainly strive toward this goal. Cannot we even learn from liberal scholarship concerning the historical and cultural background of Scripture? The denial of the principle of historical criticism can be just as mindless as the acceptance of the rationalistic philosophy of some of the higher critics.

It is my hope that those who are ecumenically oriented may also be benefited by this book, since I try to speak as one who is both evangelical and ecumenical. Many ecumenical churchmen are contributing to the polarization in the churches by falsely attributing the declines in church membership today to prophetic stands on social problems. But the call for abortion on demand, the plea for immediate, unconditional withdrawal from Indo-China, and the tacit support for the removal of censorship laws on pornography do not bear the earmarks of a prophetic stance that will go counter to the latest trends in the culture. To say the same thing that the world says and in the same way is not being true to the prophetic imperative which brings an unexpected and usually unwelcome word from God to bear on the social situation. The conciliar movement is right that the church must speak to the critical social issues of the day, but what it speaks must be a word informed by Scripture and not a political or sociological opinion. Too often ecumenists are concerned with the penultimate to the exclusion of the ultimate and therefore fail to see social problems in the light of eternity (*sub specie aeternitatis*).

The question today is whether the old wineskins of the institutional churches can hold the new wine of the movement of the Spirit. Can genuine reform and renewal be effected within the churches, or must "true believers" come out of the established churches, as D. Martyn Lloyd-Jones suggests? It is my hope that Spirit-filled Christians will stay within the church and seek to be a leavening influence. It is nonetheless true that there is also a time to separate, particularly when the doors are irrevocably closed to any earnest attempt at reform or renewal. Yet this should be done only as a last resort, and it should be deemed a sign of failure and therefore an act that calls for divine forgiveness.

The need today is for courageous Christians who are willing to suffer in their forthright witness to the truth. The great saints of the past endured intimidation and persecution not only by the world but also by the church. Yet in the knowledge that Jesus Christ is victorious over the powers of darkness the committed Christian can face the future with confidence and hope, since he knows that he is on the side that will win in the end. Luther put it this way: "Redemption occurs in hope. It is in the process of becoming. Here we must stand, fence, and deal out blows. The coward is overtaken by disaster." Would that we might recover such a robust faith for our time.

I wish to thank *Religion in Life* for permission to republish Chapter II, "The New Evangelicalism," which appeared in the Fall 1972 issue of that magazine. Chapter V on Pietism was originally given in condensed form as one of the Founders Day lectures at Bethel Seminary in Minneapolis, Minnesota, in February of 1972.

—D. B.

Contents

Strong eruptions of religious faith have always been marked by the appearance of people with firm, unapologetic, often uncompromising convictions — that is, by types that are the very opposite from those presently engaged in the various "relevance" operations . . . Put simply: Ages of faith are not marked by "dialogue" but by proclamation.

—Peter Berger

I

Introduction: The Resurgence of Evangelicalism

Signs of Evangelical Renewal

The signs are unmistakable that evangelicalism today is experiencing a definite upturn. In 1971 some twelve thousand students traveled to a weeklong Inter-Varsity missionary conference at the University of Illinois over the Easter holidays. In Dallas in June of 1972 the Campus Crusade for Christ convened nearly eighty thousand young people from seventy-five countries for a Jesus Festival. The national evangelistic campaign known as Key 73, involving several major rallies throughout the country, has been supported by nearly 140 Protestant denominations as well as American Catholic bishops. Lay witness missions in which groups of traveling laymen give public testimony to their salvation in Jesus Christ are becoming ever more popular in the mainline churches. One new denomination, the Baptist Bible Fellowship, founded only in 1950, claims a membership in the hundreds of thousands and five of America's ten largest Sunday Schools. Unfortunately its militant fundamentalism has turned it in the direction of sectarianism rather than mainstream evangelicalism. The evangelist Rex Humbard conducts his Cathedral of Tomorrow program on 360 TV stations every Sunday morning, though there are signs that he has overextended himself.

Conservative evangelical churches are gaining at a rate of 3 percent a year while liberal religious bodies are either stagnant or declining. The mainline ecumenical churches are suffering special losses, particularly in Sunday School membership. In the past five years the Methodist church lost over five hundred thousand members. The same denomination saw its Sunday School enrollment drop from 7,303,873 to 5,924,464 within a recent four-year span. In the past two years the United Presbyterian Sunday Schools have decreased by 245,000 pupils.

In Europe the steady growth of independent evangelical and millenarian churches stands in contrast to the sharp declines in membership and attendance not only in the state churches but also in the traditional free churches, such as the Methodist and Baptist. The burgeoning of evangelical student groups, such as the Inter-Varsity Fellowship in England, coupled with the deterioration of the Student Christian Movement and denominational student organizations is also indicative of an evangelical surge.

While denominational publishing houses are facing mounting deficits, it is noteworthy that evangelical companies are prospering. Several of these have recently published religious best sellers. Among the flourishing American evangelical concerns are Eerdmans, Zondervan, Word, Revell, Inter-Varsity, Moody, Creation House, Baker and Bethany Fellowship. In England we can point to the success of Inter-Varsity and Tyndale, Scripture Union, and Hodder and Stoughton's religious list. Some of the denominational publishing houses find themselves in great difficulties and are contemplating consolidation in order to survive. Roman Catholic publishing houses are also doing poorly.

Another sign of the evangelical resurgence is to be seen in the flowering of evangelical renewal movements within the mainline denominations. Here can be mentioned the Fellowship of Witness in the Episcopal Church, Lutherans Alert in the American Lutheran Church, the Fellowship of Concerned Churchmen in the United Church of Christ, the Presbyterian Lay Committee and Presbyterians for Biblical Concerns in the United Presbyterian Church, Concerned Presbyterians and Presbyterian Churchmen United in the Presbyterian Church U.S., and the Good News movement in Methodism. There are similar fellowships of spiritual renewal in the Disciples of Christ, the American Baptist Convention and the United Church of Canada.

In Europe the evangelical renaissance is reflected in the "No Other Gospel" movement in continental Lutheran and Reformed Protestantism. Several of its leaders were identified with the Confessing Church in Germany in its struggle against Hitler. In West Germany and Scandinavia a conservative Lutheran movement has arisen called "The Gathering about the Bible and Confessions." One should also take note of the thriving Church of England Evangelical Council, which is a branch of the worldwide Evangelical Fellowship in the Anglican Communion. The rise of several new free seminaries in continental Europe which stand forthrightly on biblical fundamentals is still another indication of the mounting strength of conservative evangelicalism.

The appearance of new ventures in community life of an evangelical, pietistic orientation further attests that a conservative wind is blowing.[1] We here have in mind Lee Abbey and Scargill in England; the Sisters of Mary, the Brotherhood of Christ and the Brotherhood of the Cross in Germany; the Brethren of the Common Life in Switzerland and Germany; the Sisters of Pomeyrol in France; the Daughters of Mary in Denmark and Sweden; L'Abri Fellowship in Switzerland; and Bethany Fellowship in Minnesota. Another significant experiment is Operation Mobilization, a Christian literature crusade, whose members are organized in gospel teams where there is com-

---

[1] See my forthcoming book *Wellsprings of Renewal,* to be published by Eerdmans.

plete sharing; its headquarters are in Bromley, England. The communities that have emerged out of the neo-Pentecostal and Jesus movements likewise signify a surge of new life in the "old-time religion."

Evangelical sentiment within Roman Catholicism is definitely growing, as can be seen in the Focalari, the Cursillo and the Catholic Pentecostal movements. At Notre Dame University in June of 1972 over eight thousand people associated with the charismatic awakening assembled to demonstrate their newfound unity in the Spirit. Charismatic prayer groups are becoming quite common in many Catholic parishes. In these prayer groups as in the neo-Pentecostal movement generally one can detect a tension between a spiritualistic and evangelical orientation; in the former the appeal is directed to inner experience, and in the latter it is based on Scripture.

The growth of third-force Protestantism, which embraces the sect groups, and the emergence of the Jesus movement also signify that conservative religion is on the uprise. In the third force we include the Pentecostals, the Holiness churches, the Plymouth Brethren, the Bible churches, the Seventh-Day Adventists and the Churches of Christ. We do not include the cults such as the Jehovah's Witnesses, the Spiritists and the Mormons, which are likewise experiencing rapid growth. The so-called third force comprises the growing edge of Protestantism today; this is especially evident in South America, Africa and Asia.

Looking at the European scene, the Pentecostals now comprise the largest of the Protestant free churches in the Scandinavian countries, though their rate of increase has slowed down considerably. In Spain the Plymouth Brethren are the most numerous of the Protestant bodies, and the Pentecostals are the largest in Italy. Seventh-Day Adventists show considerable strength in such countries as Romania, Yugoslavia and Finland. In Russia evangelical Baptists enjoy continuing growth and remarkable vitality amid great difficulties. The Baptist Church in Romania is also prospering and now claims 120,000 registered members. Sect groups like the New Apostolic Church and the Jehovah's Witnesses have had spectacularly high growth rates; the strength of the former is mainly limited to West Germany and Switzerland.

Additional evidences for the evangelical resurgence are abundant. The Graham crusades have lost none of their impact, and healing revivals are increasing in popularity. The relative prosperity of the independent evangelical seminaries such as Asbury, Dallas, Gordon-Conwell and Fuller,[2] and the sound financial health of evangelical magazines like *Christianity Today, Eternity* and *Christian Life* are surely indicative of a new mood in American religion. It is well to note that *The Christian Century,* standard-bearer of liberal Protestantism, is beset by financial woes because of rising costs and dropping circulation. Even the one-time conservative *Christian Herald* has suffered a noticeable decline in subscriptions parallel with its evolving moderate stance. It is also interesting to contrast the failing fortunes of the *Presbyterian Survey* (which has recently lost 100,000 readers) with the prospering evangelical *Presbyterian Journal* (which has gained nearly 20,000). The steady rise in the number of missionaries in evangelical churches and mission societies coupled with the startling reduction in the missionary force in the mainline churches is likewise significant. An evangelical church, unlike a liberal church, will have a passion to convert the world.

In the inner city of London it is interesting to observe that among the very few churches that are presently well attended on Sunday mornings and evenings are All Souls' Church, pastored by a staff of evangelical Anglicans including Dr. John R. W. Stott, and Westminster Chapel,

[2] Trinity Evangelical Divinity School in Deerfield, Illinois, which has an interdenominational faculty but which is officially associated with the Evangelical Free Church, has also shown amazing growth and vigor. Trinity stands somewhat to the right of Fuller and Gordon-Conwell.

an independent Congregational church whose pastor was for many years Dr. Martyn Lloyd-Jones, staunch evangelical Calvinist. Since the retirement of Dr. Lloyd-Jones the attendance at Westminster Chapel has slipped, but it still exceeds that of most other London churches.

Dean M. Kelley contends in his very relevant book *Why Conservative Churches Are Growing* that people today are yearning for a clear purpose in life, for definite answers to the riddle of existence.[3] They are more engrossed in the quest for meaning in life than in social reform. Conservative churches seek to meet these deep spiritual needs while liberal churches seem to be more interested in working for social change.

Some Dangers

When evangelicalism becomes respectable and even fashionable, then the temptation to accommodate to the values and goals of the world becomes almost overwhelming. That such an accommodation is present in many circles of evangelicalism should remind us that the current renewal of religious conservatism is not without its dangers. Indeed, one can ask whether the evangelical renaissance is rooted in a profound spiritual awakening or in the counter-revolution of middle America against the vagaries of the New Left.

Some critics of evangelicalism are warning of the emergence of a new American civil religion in which fervent and often blind patriotism is combined with loyalty to the Puritan ethic and religious tenets associated with the "old-time religion." There is nothing wrong with trying to bring a Christian presence into the affairs of state, but there is reason for concern if this tends to impede prophetic criticism of the state. Unfortunately many of those who decry the principle of civil religion are seemingly blind to the threat of a militant secularism that

[3] See Dean M. Kelley, *Why Conservative Churches Are Growing* (N.Y.: Harper, 1972).

seeks the removal of religious values and concerns from the public domain. On the European scene, where evangelicals are very much in a minority, the temptation of an alliance with the political establishment does not present itself except possibly in Northern Ireland and Norway. This temptation is very real, however, in South Africa.

Among the specific pitfalls which evangelicals must guard against is the heresy of easy salvation, what Bonhoeffer called "cheap grace." Too often in the ranks of evangelicalism salvation is made to appear almost too simple, as a momentary experience instead of a lifelong struggle. Grace is free, but it is also costly: it demands from its beneficiaries their very lives. Repentance is commonly preached, but it is sometimes forgotten that true revival entails repentance for social as well as personal sins. The revival among the Sisters of Mary in Darmstadt, Germany, can be deemed authentic, since these women were moved to turn to Christ partly out of guilt for the crimes of their people against the Jews.

The contemporary charismatic revival contains much that can be commended, and yet too often in this movement people seek for Pentecost without first bowing before Calvary. Faith is widely viewed as simply a preparation for "the baptism of the Holy Spirit," which is seen as proof or evidence of the presence of God in one's life. This is not to deny the truth that there are special blessings of the Holy Spirit subsequent to conversion; one must not rest content with the indwelling of the Spirit but go on to be filled with the Spirit. Yet there is reason for concern when we seek for the security of evidential signs of the gift of the Spirit. Francis Schaeffer rightly warns of a "super-spirituality" in which extraordinary experiences figure more highly than obedience to the gospel.

The idea of instant sanctification is another doctrinal deviation associated with the Pentecostal and neo-Pentecostal awakenings. The Assemblies of God prefers to speak of progressive sanctification instead of the blessing of total sanctification. The Pentecostal Mülheim Association of Christian Fellowships in Germany warns against the pitfalls of perfectionism and also disputes the view that the baptism of the Spirit can be separated from the experience of conversion.

John Wesley, whose ideas on sanctification have made a definite impact upon the modern Holiness and Pentecostal movements, assured his hearers that the only perfection attainable in this life is a relative perfection, one in which we still must seek for the mercy and power of Almighty God. According to him, even the most saintly of Christians can never be free from involuntary transgressions.

Dr. A. W. Tozer, one of the guiding lights of the Christian and Missionary Alliance, was constantly alert to the peril of instant salvation: "By trying to pack all of salvation into one experience, or two, the advocates of instant Christianity flaunt the law of development which runs through all nature. They ignore the sanctifying effects of suffering, cross carrying and practical obedience."[4]

The Puritan tradition was very much aware of man's inveterate desire for an easy road to salvation and sanctification. Samuel Rutherford held that "the best regenerate have their defilements, and . . . there will be the filth of sin in their hearts to the end. Glory alone will make our hearts pure and perfect, never till then will they be absolutely sinless."[5] In the view of Jonathan Edwards: "The Scriptures everywhere represent the seeking, the striving, and the labour of a Christian as being chiefly to be gone through *after* his conversion, and his conversion as being but the beginning of the work." As the Puritans saw it, there are no automatic guarantees for salvation.

---

[4] A. W. Tozer, *That Incredible Christian* (Harrisburg, Pa.: Christian Publications, 1964), p. 25.

[5] Alexander Whyte, *Samuel Rutherford and Some of his Correspondents* (London: Oliphant, Anderson & Ferrier, 1894), pp. 177, 178.

On the contrary we are called to persevere in faith amid great trial and tribulation.

Another sign of cultural accommodation is the appearance of a rationalistic biblicism in which an appeal is made to the axioms of formal logic or the evidences of the senses to buttress the claims of biblical faith. A few conservative scholars today even go so far as to hold that the resurrection of Christ can be rationally proved to the natural man. When an absolute identification is made between the words of the biblical text and the truth of revelation, then the doorway is opened to rationalism, since this means that God's Word becomes accessible to natural reason. It is interesting to note that Francis Schaeffer, who seeks to make a place for reason prior to faith, has been accused of apriorism and neglecting "factual evidence and theistic argument" in one of his recent books.[6] It is possible to hold to the divine inspiration of Scripture and even the infallibility of Scripture without reducing its truth to a datum available to human perception. Luther, who certainly affirmed the divine authority of Scripture, nevertheless contended: "Faith directs itself towards the things that are invisible. Indeed, only when that which is believed on is hidden, can it provide an opportunity for faith."

Hand in hand with this rationalistic emphasis often goes an anti-theological bias. In conservative circles one can detect a notable dependence on the findings of psychology and secular philosophy while in secular, liberal theology an appeal is made to sociology and political science. Yet theology, the doctrinal exposition of Holy Scripture, is often regarded with mistrust; but this betrays a markedly cultural orientation in which the authority of reason is substituted for that of revelation. A great many conservative evangelicals today are exceedingly troubled by the lack of solid theological substance in

[6] See *Christian Scholar's Review,* Vol. I, No. 4 (Summer, 1971), p. 371.

evangelical writing, and some also have grave reservations about an apologetics that builds upon a criterion held in common with secular thought.

Still another hazard that confronts evangelical theology is ghettoism. This takes the form of the interiorization of piety, thereby isolating the Christian from the critical issues of the time. Elton Trueblood has criticized the Jesus movement for its privatism and individualism, which prevent it from rendering a potent social witness. In his words: "A genuine gospel will always be concerned with human justice rather than the mere cultivation of a warm inner glow."[7]

Ghettoism is also present in the form of sectarianism in which Christians are called to come out of the apostate churches and start holy clubs of their own. Such groups easily fall victim to the legalism of taboos in which visible marks of separation are drawn between Christians and their worldly neighbors. Unfortunately very often in these circles much is made of the evils of dancing, cosmetics, drinking and card-playing, but very little is said about the sins of racial injustice and the exploitation of the poor by rapacious landlords and unscrupulous business concerns. It was against a callous legalism that Zinzendorf was led to remark that the discipleship of Christ should not be seen as "legalistic duty" but instead as "our life" and "our joy."[8]

In order to bolster their own particular interpretation of a biblical doctrine many evangelicals expend their energies in demolishing the positions of fellow-evangelicals who might differ on some point or other. Evangelicals need to engage in dialogue and so learn from one another if we are to present a unified and effectual witness to the world. Consigning our opponent to the camp of the enemy simply because he cannot accept our

[7] *Yokefellows International*, Vol. XII, No. 4 (Dec., 1971), p. 2.

[8] Arthur Mettler, "Count Zinzendorf" in *The Plough*, Vol. V, No. 3 (1957) [pp. 71-75], p. 75.

own pet theory of predestination or biblical inspiration is an affront to Christian charity and does a disservice to the cause of Christian unity. It is necessary, of course, to be clear in our minds on what is fundamental and what is peripheral, but even in disagreement on basic matters we must approach those who hold a contrary view in the spirit of Christian love. And certainly among our evangelical brethren we should emphasize the things that unite us rather than those that divide us.

Then there is the temptation of an arid traditionalism in which a call is sounded to return to the beliefs and practices of our forefathers. This too can be a form of culture-religion, for it often entails absolutizing the attitudes and mores of a particular period in history. Many evangelicals seem content simply to lean upon the confessional statements of past ages without realizing that the times in which we live call for new confessions as well as biblically grounded innovations in worship and missionary methods. New confessions are always necessary because the church is constantly threatened by new heresies. According to Barth confessions become necessary "when a man realizes that . . . the faith of the Christian community is confronted or questioned from within or without by the phenomena of unbelief, superstition and heresy."[9] Are not we living in such times now?

Pelagianism is also a constant temptation, especially when faith becomes worldly. The synergistic idea that man helps to procure divine justification has been especially rampant in latter-day revivalism. The revivalist Sam Jones declared: "You convert yourself, and when you convert yourself, God regenerates you."[10] Finney preached a sermon titled "Sinners Bound to Change Their Own Hearts," which stands in marked contrast to the

[9] Karl Barth, *Church Dogmatics*, III, 4. Eds. G. W. Bromiley and T. F. Torrance (Edinburgh: T. & T. Clark, 1961), pp. 78, 79.

[10] William G. McLoughlin, Jr., *Modern Revivalism* (N.Y.: Ronald Press, 1959), p. 291.

much publicized sermon of Jonathan Edwards, "Sinners in the Hands of an Angry God." At their best the revivalists, including Finney, sought to hold in balance the gift of divine grace and the obligation of man to make an active response to grace, but this tension was often sundered when an overreliance was placed on techniques and schemes to induce conversions.

This brings us finally to the carnality and frivolity in much modern-day popular evangelical religion. This can be seen in the glorification of beauty queens and athletes who happen to be Christian. It is also noticeable in the fascination of many evangelicals with public relations and showmanship. In some schools and churches technique and method are valued more highly than right doctrine, and group dynamics is given more attention than prayer and other spiritual disciplines. The popularity of gospel rock groups that appeal to the sensual side of man is yet another indication of accommodation to worldly standards. Culture-religion is also evident in the camaraderie between some evangelical leaders and right-wing politicians.

Dr. Tozer scores the culture-religion in modern evangelicalism:

> The flaw in current evangelism lies in its humanistic approach. It struggles to be supernaturalistic but never quite makes it. It is frankly fascinated by the great, noisy, aggressive world with its big name, its hero worship, its wealth and its garish pageantry. To the millions of disappointed persons who have always yearned for worldly glory but never attained to it, the modern evangel offers a quick and easy shortcut to their heart's desire. Peace of mind, happiness, prosperity, social acceptance, publicity, success in sports, business, the entertainment field, and perchance to sit occasionally at the same banquet table with a celebrity—all this on earth and heaven at last. Certainly no insurance company can offer half as much.[11]

[11] A. W. Tozer, *Born After Midnight* (Harrisburg, Pa.: Christian Publications, 1959), p. 22.

In reacting to the fusion of faith and political and cultural conservatism some evangelicals go to the opposite extreme of identifying the cause of Christ with women's liberation, social revolution, progressive education, sensitivity training and other fads of the New Left. They also occasionally fall into the liberal error of equating evangelism and social action, but this proves to be simply another variety of culture-Christianity.

With all the emphasis on mass crusades and rallies today it is well to remember that Jesus sometimes fled from the crowds. His ministry as well as that of his apostles was singularly free from ostentation and flamboyancy. Much is said today in evangelical circles about evangelism and church growth but very little on the spiritual life, prayer and asceticism. Both kinds of activity, of course, are necessary, but can there ever be a permanent and authentic spiritual awakening that is not nurtured and grounded in prayer? To the credit of the Billy Graham team they have sought to prepare for their evangelistic forays by weeks of concerted prayer.

Karl Barth has some wise words on the dangers of culture-Christianity:

> Christianity knows itself at least more akin to ascetics and pietists, strange though their behaviour may be, than to "healthy, evangelical national piety." . . . Christianity displays a certain inclination to side with those who are immature, sullen, and depressed, with those who "come off badly" and are, in consequence, ready for revolution.[12]

Barth, of course, sees violent revolution as a false answer, but he does perceive that the poor who are ready for such a revolution are often more open to the gospel than the rich and self-satisfied.

---

12 Karl Barth, *The Epistle to the Romans*. Trans. from the 6th ed. by Edwyn C. Hoskyns (London: Oxford Univ. Press, 1933), p. 463.

Signs of Hope

Though the danger of culture-religion is very real in the current resurgence of evangelicalism, there are also signs of hope. One of these is the rediscovery of the social implications of the gospel on the part of many evangelical leaders today. Hear these words of Paul S. Rees of World Vision: "Our evangelical extreme of silence, passivity—and sometimes complicity—where the rooted social evils of our time are concerned is no answer to the extreme of the radical social activists who seem so prone to mute the gospel."[13] Carl Henry in his book *A Plea for Evangelical Demonstration* argues cogently for the need to hold evangelism and social action in balance. A similar note is sounded by Frederick Schroeder in his *Visions and Renewal*, in which he contends that "personal regeneration and social reconstruction must go hand in hand."[14] Leighton Ford in a crusade in Rochester, New York, in 1972 voiced the plea for Christians to become involved in prison reform. He also announced that a long-term volunteer program has been established to assist prisoners at Attica.

Signs of growing discontent with the immoralities of warfare can also be detected in evangelical circles. Lewis Smedes, Professor of Theology at Fuller Seminary, has upbraided the evangelical church for its strange silence on the mass bombing of Vietnam. He contends that such bombing "is a spiritual issue," since it imperils the livelihood of the civilian population. The awareness of the church to such devastation "is a barometer of its spiritual sensitivity" to the broader spectrum of moral questions.[15] Lewis Smedes and his colleague James Daane as well as Mark Hatfield and Tom Skinner are becoming

---

[13] In *World Vision*, Vol. XVI, No. 4 (April, 1972), p. 23.

[14] Frederick W. Schroeder, *Visions and Renewal* (St. Louis: Eden Publishing House, 1972), p. 68.

[15] In *The Reformed Journal*, Vol. XXII, No. 7 (Sept., 1972), p. 3.

increasingly vocal opponents of war, racism and poverty.

It is becoming recognized that the changed heart, though the foundation for a new society, must be united with the discerning mind. Men and women who have been converted from personal sin must also become sensitive to social evils and aspire to correct them. A changed heart involves a change in spiritual perspective, in desires and goals, but does not necessarily entail an alteration in political and economic attitudes, at least not immediately. Bernard Ramm makes this astute comment: "The assurances so frequently given from the pulpit that if we can change enough hearts we will change society cannot be entirely believed. . . . More is needed in our present situation than changed hearts. There must be just programs and righteous policies."[16] It is commonly said that legislation is not the answer to social ills but conversion. Yet legislation is a proximate answer even as conversion is the ultimate answer. The gospel and law go together, and one apart from the other results in a truncated spiritual vision.

Another sign of hope today is the mounting reaction of younger evangelicals to obscurantism, especially in the area of the doctrine of Scripture. The International Fellowship of Evangelical Students has issued a statement rejecting "wooden literalism" and "divine dictation." The document does assert that "Scripture is entirely trustworthy" in all that it teaches. H. M. Kuitert in his *Do You Understand What You Read?* refers to the "timebound" character of the Bible, though he also speaks of the timeless character of its message. The concept of inerrancy is now seen in some quarters as a shibboleth used to promote party unity, yet we would caution that the basic truth in this concept not be disregarded. Against those who would elevate the Bible unduly Carl Henry has

[16] Bernard Ramm, *The Right, the Good and the Happy* (Waco, Texas: Word Books, 1971), pp. 157, 158.

declared in a recent article that the final authority for the
Christian is the living God Himself, though he also criticizes those who relish finding errors in the Bible.[17] It is
coming to be recognized that Scripture bears the imprint
of human frailty as well as the stamp of divine infallibility.

In some ultraconservative circles today the dominant
issue is still the defense of a naive biblical literalism, but
this is not the front where the battle should be waged. We
as evangelicals are, of course, bound to the original or
literal meaning of the text, but we must allow for the fact
that the writer may sometimes intend his testimony to be
taken symbolically. The threat that must be faced is a
humanistic naturalism that denies a priori the very possibility of divine action in history and therefore of any
kind of miracle whatsoever. But conservatives must not
get trapped in the embarrassing position of making the
credibility of the Bible rest upon the edibility of Jonah.
The new evangelicalism is shifting the battle to the right
front.

It is also encouraging to see evangelicals acknowledge
the need for returning to the central themes of the faith
and not get bogged down in controversies on peripheral
matters. Again we should listen to Carl Henry:

> To the forefront of pulpit proclamation fundamentalists
> increasingly elevated emphases that, though they are signifi-
> cant in the total context of Christian faith, do not stand in
> the forefront of apostolic preaching. Here one thinks not
> only of the virgin birth but also of biblical inerrancy—themes
> that stress the *how* more than the *what* and *why* of the
> incarnation and of the inspiration of the Word of God.[18]

Evangelicalism can stay the tide of irrationalism and
subjectivism by emphasizing the particularity and objectivity of the historical revelation in Jesus Christ. The
objectivity of God is stoutly affirmed by theologians like

[17] Carl Henry, "Evangelicals and the Bible" in *Christianity Today*, Vol.
XVI, No. 11 (March 3, 1972), pp. 35, 36.
[18] In *Christianity Today*, Vol. XVI, No. 9 (Feb. 4, 1972), p. 23.

Francis Schaeffer, who upholds "the God who is there." At the same time evangelicals would do well to eschew the opposite danger of objectivism, for the God of the Bible is not available to human perception but can only be discerned by faith.

The resurgence of evangelicalism can have favorable ecumenical implications, even though evangelicals are noted for their biting criticisms of the organized ecumenical movement. They remind us that church union can never be achieved on a political or sociological basis but only on one that is theological. Hans Urs von Balthasar describes the position of Karl Barth, who has had a notable influence on the new evangelical theology: "As he saw it, church reunion must be a union in faith, an agreement on clearly formulated articles of faith. The Churches will accomplish this through a more authentic, more vital belief, not a leveling off or a scaling down of dogmatic differences."[19]

What we should seek for today is a social evangelicalism over an exclusively individualistic evangelicalism. Such a position will not deny the priority of personal salvation but will seek to relate this to the nurture and fellowship of the church and to the areas of service in the world, including the political and economic. We should also aim for a catholic evangelicalism over a narrowly conservative evangelicalism. The key to Christian renewal today is not to be found in a repristination of conservative orthodoxy, even though renewal will not come apart from a rebirth of authentic orthodoxy. Nor should earnest Christians seek to avoid a confessional stance even while being alive to the perils of a rigid confessionalism. The hope of the church certainly does not lie in new strategies, programs and techniques. Instead it lies in a rediscovery of the catholic and evangelical roots of the faith and in an attempt to apply these to the critical social issues of our time.

[19] Hans Urs von Balthasar, *The Theology of Karl Barth* (N.Y.: Holt, Rinehart & Winston, 1971), p. 4.

II
The New Evangelicalism

The New Mood

Within the past few years a new mood can be detected in conservative circles, one that can be called "the new evangelicalism." This movement is wider and deeper than the original surge of "neo-evangelicalism," which was limited mainly to those who were seeking to eschew the excesses of fundamentalism but at the same time remain solidly biblical. Carl Henry voiced the prevailing issue at that time: "May not evangelical Christianity, dissatisfied with both fundamentalism and modernism, transcend the alternatives of the modernist fundamentalist controversy?" Since then, however, many other theologians have been attracted to an evangelical alternative to neo-orthodoxy and neo-liberalism; some of these men have come out of neo-orthodoxy and even Roman Catholicism. In addition there is a new appreciation of Pietism and Puritanism among both conservative and liberal churchmen, and this too seems to be creating a favorable climate for the new evangelical wind. One can say that the new evangelicalism is the fruit of a convergence of theological currents, though the tradition of evangelical revivalism is the dominant one.

Besides those who were identified with the earlier phase of this movement, such as Carl Henry, Bernard

Ramm and Edward Carnell, it can be said to include the following: Robert Blaikie, Marvin Anderson, Addison Leitch, Lloyd Kalland, Kenneth Hamilton, Ronald Nash, Harold Kuhn, James Perry Martin, I. John Hesselink, James Daane, Daniel Fuller, George E. Ladd, Vernon Grounds, Lewis Smedes, John Mackay, Eugene Oster-haven, Samuel Mikolaski, Vernard Eller, Dewey Beegle, Jack Rogers, Ford Lewis Battles, Arthur Holmes, David Wells, J. Rodman Williams, Donald G. Miller, Philip Watson and Elton Trueblood. (Many others, including the present author, could also probably be listed here.) On the European scene it is reflected in varying degrees in the recent writings of Hans-Joachim Kraus, Helmut Saake, J. W. Winterhager, Gordon Rupp, Hans Küng, Edmund Schlink, Mother Basilea (Klara) Schlink, Klaas Runia, Jacques Ellul, Hendrikus Berkhof, Helmut Thie-licke, H. M. Kuitert, G. C. Berkouwer, F. F. Bruce, John R. W. Stott, Colin Brown, Peter Beyerhaus and Walter Künneth. Künneth and Beyerhaus are among those who are actively involved in the "No Other Gospel" move-ment. Some of these men should be placed on the bound-ary of the new evangelicalism, but what is significant is that they are moving in this direction. Even a thinker like Ellul, who has been greatly influenced by Karl Barth, nevertheless represents a somewhat different spirit in his emphasis on personal conversion and his incisive critique of communism and social activism. Though Malcolm Muggeridge cannot be classified as an evangelical as such, his book *Jesus Rediscovered* has given much impetus to the surge of evangelical piety. The Graham crusades, the Catholic Pentecostals, the Catholic Cursillo movement, Campus Crusade for Christ and the Jesus movement are likewise contributing to the evangelical renaissance. The newly emerging evangelical theology is making itself felt not only at seminaries like Fuller, Bethel and Gordon-Conwell but also in some of the mainline denominational schools.

Consideration should also be given to Francis Schaeffer, founder of the L'Abri community in Switzerland, which has become an evangelical lighthouse in the sea of European nihilism. Though Schaeffer still has a foot in the old fundamentalism, his intense social concern and his critique of the lovelessness that afflicts many ortho- dox Christians make him a fresh voice on the evangelical scene. Of special significance is his call for "Christian revolutionaries" who will defy the status quo of the conservative religious establishment.

This latest wave of evangelicalism is distinguished by locating the authority for faith in Jesus Christ, the center of the Bible and the head of the church. As John R. W. Stott has well put it, the Bible as well as the sacraments are the divinely given signposts that direct our attention away from themselves to Christ.[1] The Bible like the sacrament is a dependent norm, since it relies for its efficacy on the Spirit of Christ; but against some strands of neo-orthodoxy these men are saying that the Bible is also a dependable norm, i.e., it gives a reliable and trust- worthy witness to Jesus Christ.

In stressing the authority of the divine revelation dis- closed in the Bible and culminating in Jesus Christ, the new evangelicals seek to counteract the skepticism and eclecticism that mar much of the current theological scene, including the ecumenical movement. They agree with the neo-orthodox that there is no certain knowledge of God apart from His self-revelation in Jesus Christ, but they go on to contend that there is no salvation apart from personal faith in the living Christ.

The new evangelicals look not only to the Protestant Reformation for their spiritual and theological illumina- tion but also to the spiritual movements of purification subsequent to the Reformation: Pietism, Puritanism and Evangelicalism. A Calvinistic strain is very much present in neo-evangelicalism, but this is only one of several

---

[1] See John R. W. Stott, *Christ the Controversialist* (London: Tyndale, 1970), pp. 101-103.

theological currents. The Wesleyan note can also be heard, and even Catholic mysticism is represented.

Among the theologians of the church who figure prominently in the writings of the evangelical renewalists are Calvin, Luther, Wesley, Kierkegaard, Pascal, Abraham Kuyper and Peter Forsyth. Also worthy of mention are such luminaries of Puritanism as Jonathan Edwards, Richard Baxter, John Owen and Samuel Rutherford; among the Pietists who are coming to be appreciated are Philip Spener, Count Zinzendorf, Tersteegen and the Blumhardts. It is interesting to note that quotations from Spener and Zinzendorf are beginning to appear in *Decision* magazine, the voice of the Billy Graham Evangelistic Association. Still other men of piety and wisdom who are highly regarded are William Booth, Charles Simeon, Charles Spurgeon, Oswald Chambers, James Orr, Karl Heim, O. Hallesby and A. W. Tozer. Tozer, like many of the early Pietists, often appealed to the mystics of the Catholic church for support. Some recent figures on the theological scene who seem to be exerting an influence upon the movement are Karl Barth, C. S. Lewis, Emil Brunner and Dietrich Bonhoeffer. It is not Bonhoeffer's *Letters and Papers from Prison* but rather his *Life Together* and his *The Cost of Discipleship* (*Nachfolge*) that are attracting special attention.

Salient Notes

Foremost among the salient notes of the new evangelicalism is the divine authority of Scripture. It was to be expected that the doctrine of Scripture would be of paramount importance in this movement, but especially significant is the fact that this is not a recrudescence of fundamentalism. Unlike the fundamentalists the new evangelicals tend to accept the principle of historical criticism of Scripture (cf. George Eldon Ladd's *The New Testament and Criticism*). They also acknowledge that the Bible is the word of man as well as the Word of God and that the divine Word is made known through a human word that bears the marks of cultural conditioning. It is becoming recognized that it is inadmissible to posit a pure, distilled Word of God free from all human traces. The infallibility and inerrancy of Scripture are generally adhered to, but these old concepts are being reinterpreted. It is now said in many circles that the teaching or doctrine of the Bible is without error rather than everything reported in the Bible. (Here Kenneth Kantzer and Clark Pinnock would very likely concur.) The message of the Bible is said to be infallible, not the text itself; this message, moreover, is available to man only by the Holy Spirit. The new evangelicals are adamant in their contention, however, that the revealed Word of God, Jesus Christ, must not be set against the written Word, that the latter is the original and definitive witness to Jesus Christ.

Another characteristic mark of this movement is its stress upon the rationality of faith. For these men revelation is both experiential and conceptual; it is both personal and propositional. This is to say that we have the truth of God in human affirmations and human testimony, though this is not to imply that the statements themselves are identical with the very Word of God. Some of the avant-garde evangelicals seek to affirm a dynamic theory of revelation without denying that revelation is word as well as act.

Father Hans Küng, who is moving toward an evangelical position, maintains that the faith of the church is dependent on articles or propositions of faith. He rejects the idea of guaranteed infallible statements or pronouncements, but he does not deny that propositions may become infallible by the grace of God, that they may indeed convey infallible truth. Unlike most of the new evangelicals his emphasis is upon the humanity over the divinity of Scripture, but he also seems to affirm that Scripture attests and carries the infallible truth of revelation and salvation. His evangelical orientation is especially evident in his appeal to the message of Scripture over the historical consciousness of the church.

Most of the evangelical renewalists hold that faith is not dependent on metaphysics, though a few see the need to work out the metaphysical implications of the faith. Unlike those conservatives who tend toward a Christian rationalism, such as John W. Montgomery, Clark Pinnock and Francis Schaeffer, many of the new breed of evangelicals seem closer to Abraham Kuyper, who affirmed that faith is not the outcome of demonstration or observation and who called for the freedom of theology from philosophy.[2] In contradistinction to existentialist theology they contend that faith is not a leap in the dark but a rational commitment to the Divine Light present in Jesus Christ and reflected in sacred Scripture. Faith is cognitive, not noncognitive or less than cognitive; though it does not give perfect knowledge, it does give valid, authentic knowledge of God and His purposes for the world.

The new evangelicalism is also distinguished by its recognition of the realities of regeneration and sanctification. It is not enough to be pardoned of sin; one must be cleansed of sin and thereby equipped to live a new and victorious life. The Christian life is deemed just as significant as Christian doctrine. Evangelicals true to their Puritan heritage see the need not only for orthodoxy but also for "orthopraxis" (right living). Their intention is to uphold both personal morality and "social holiness" (John Wesley). While moralism is censured, Christian practice is considered the indispensable fruit of a living faith.

Again, the new evangelical movement insists on the need for personal faith in Jesus Christ for salvation. It declares itself against the doctrine of a final universal

---

[2] Though having a different methodology from men like Schaeffer and Pinnock, I share with them a firm fidelity to the faith once delivered to the saints. I also share the deep social concern of all these men and have benefited from their writings.

salvation, though it does not necessarily oppose the concept of a universal atonement, as did the older Calvinism. Christ died for all men, but His death is beneficial only to those who believe.

There is also to be seen in this progressive conservatism a definite eschatological interest, and this might appear to ally it with the current theology of hope. But in contrast to the theologians of hope (Moltmann, Pannenberg, Braaten, Metz), the mainline evangelicals do not see a kingdom of God in the temporal future but instead a new heaven and a new earth created by supernatural intervention. They look forward to the personal, visible coming of Jesus Christ that will bring down the curtain on world history and usher in the new aeon. While the theologians of hope also point to a new creation of God in the future, they are prone to interpret this in terms of the "historifying" of the cosmos rather than eternity breaking into time or a kingdom beyond history. It should be noted that there is among the new evangelicals a marked aversion to dispensationalism and a movement away from the apocalyptic speculation that has characterized premillennial fundamentalism; some, however, still hold to a premillennial position.

Finally the new conservatives tend to underscore the spiritual mission of the church. The primary aim of the church is to preach the gospel and to make disciples of Jesus Christ. Social service is an integral though not the primary part of this mission; political action on the other hand is a fruit or consequence rather than an essential part of the church's mission. While not averse to political action and social change, the new evangelicals speak of the prior need for personal regeneration as the prerequisite to any lasting social benefits. Jacques Ellul reflects this general position when he contends (in his *The Meaning of the City*) that the answer to social sin is not reforms first but individual and collective repentance.

It is heartening to note among some of the new breed of evangelicals a recognition of the social dimension of

Christianity, which must not be neglected or obscured. These people recoil from creating a new Social Gospel, but they nevertheless hold that it is necessary to rediscover the social implications of the biblical gospel. Dr. Gilbert James of Asbury Seminary struck a salutary note when he warned in his address at the Second Convocation of the evangelical Good News movement (Methodist) in Cincinnati (July, 1971) that conversion which is induced by the techniques of high-powered evangelism is often skin-deep and that true conversion must bear fruit in social concern and action.

Differences from Neo-Orthodoxy

The new evangelicals have been influenced to some degree by the luminaries of neo-orthodoxy, but it is not unduly difficult to discern some important differences. In the first place the former stress regeneration and sanctification over justification. It is not the justification of the ungodly, which formed the basic motif in the Lutheran Reformation and also in neo-orthodoxy, but the sanctification of the righteous that is given the most attention.

An equally sharp divergence is apparent in the attitudes to the immanental dimension in God's activity. Though they agree with the neo-orthodox that God is essentially transcendent, the evangelical renewalists are quick to point to the fact that He comes to man in Jesus Christ and that He indwells those who have faith. This is not an incarnational immanentism as in Roman and Anglo-Catholicism nor an immanentism of interpersonal relationships as in neo-liberalism but an immanentism of the Holy Spirit. Like the Pietists and Puritans the new evangelicals are prone to quote from Paul: "Christ in you, the hope of glory" (Col. 1:27). The stress is upon the inner life; social service is seen as an inevitable product of inner sanctification.

While theologians like Barth, Brunner and Reinhold Niebuhr were emphatic in their praise of the gift of

Christian freedom, and incisive in their invective against legalism, the new conservatives are beginning to speak of the need for spiritual disciplines. Indeed, it is coming to be recognized that freedom can be realized only through service and obedience. A word of caution must be uttered here, since not all conservatives make this particular emphasis, but such men as John Mackay, John Stott, E. Stanley Jones, Harold Lindsell, Elton Trueblood and Philip Watson are very insistent on the need for a disciplined, interior life.

Again, the new evangelicals are closer to particularism than universalism. They are adamant that there can be no true or full salvation apart from conscious personal commitment to Jesus Christ. The dialectic theology, on the other hand, often spoke of the "hidden Christ," the "latent church" or the world as the invisible church. Against Barthianism the new evangelicalism insists that men are not already saved in Christ but that they can be saved because of the offer of salvation made through the preaching of the gospel. Whereas for the neo-orthodox the response of faith is generally seen as basically ethical, the evangelical conservatives see it as soteriological as well.

While neo-orthodox theology was marked by a profound distrust of religious experience, the neo-evangelicals see the experience of faith as an integral part of faith itself. Faith is not simply trust in the promises of God in Scripture but an experience of the living Christ who makes His dwelling place in our hearts. It also contains the notes of assurance and confidence. The ground of faith, however, is not experience but the revelation of God in biblical history culminating in Jesus Christ. The experiential dimension of faith was not denied by neo-orthodox theologians, but their emphasis was on the risk in faith and the leap of faith rather on an abiding inner communion with the divine Savior.

This renewal movement within evangelicalism is inclined to be dualistic rather than monistic. While Barth and Bonhoeffer spoke as if the whole world were now the kingdom of Christ, the evangelicals see two kingdoms at war with one another—the kingdom of God and the kingdom of Satan. The devil and his hosts have been overthrown by the cross of Christ, but they are not reconciled servants of Christ (as Cullmann, for example, maintains) but rather rebels against the rule of Christ. God accomplishes His will in a secret way through the devil and in spite of the devil, but this is not to suppose that the devil is now an agent of the kingdom of God. The new evangelicals also have difficulty with Barth's contention that the devil has no positive power, that his power is now only in the minds of men. This seems to minimize the dire threat of evil in the world.

As in Protestant orthodoxy and fundamentalism, the inspiration of Scripture plays an important role in the thinking of many progressive evangelicals. At the same time they take pains to guard against any mechanical theory of inspiration and seek to do justice to the humanity of the Scriptural authors. Calvin's conception of the Holy Spirit accommodating Himself to the culture and thought-forms of the human authors of Scripture is given much weight in present-day evangelical discussions. The neo-orthodox theologians spoke much of revelation but very little of inspiration. Barth is an exception and even includes the words of the biblical authors in the event of inspiration. Yet he has been reluctant to affirm that inspiration guarantees a fully reliable and true account of the works of God in biblical history.

While the neo-orthodox preferred to speak of the transcendence of God, they were often unwilling to affirm His supernatural intervention in the processes of nature. Those who were oriented toward existentialism were prone to see God more as Subject than Agent, the One who acts in nature and history. With the exception of Barth the neo-orthodox tended to play down the miracles of Jesus, and many even cast doubt upon His corporeal resurrection from the grave. The new evangelicals are very open to the concept of the "supernatural," though they acknowledge that it needs to be reinterpreted (see Kenneth Hamilton's *Revolt Against Heaven* and Robert Blaikie's *'Secular Christianity' and God Who Acts*). Unlike the fundamentalists, however, they have marked reservations about using the biblical miracles for apologetic purposes. They would be inclined to say that the miracles of Christ attested His divinity to those with the eyes to see but by no means proved it.

Both neo-orthodox theologians and neo-evangelicals have basically a futuristic eschatology though the latter stress the personal, visible return of Christ. Again, while the Barthians, for example, speak of the second advent as a revelation of what has already taken place at Calvary, the new conservatives tend to see it as the culmination and fulfillment of the work of Christ.

Like Brunner and Niebuhr and unlike Barth and Bonhoeffer, the new evangelicals have a marked apologetic interest. They remind us that authentic conversion entails the persuasion of the mind and that genuine proclamation does not cancel out all argumentation. But they are reluctant to return to the rationalistic apologetics of the older orthodoxy even as they seek to make a place for the confounding of unbelief in the light of the gospel. Some of these men would be open to Barth's remark: "Dogmatics too . . . has to speak all along the line as faith opposing unbelief, and to that extent all along the line its language must be apologetic, polemical."[3] What Barth opposes is an "intended apologetic," one that seeks to base the case for Christianity on a criterion held in common with unbelief. The more biblically astute among the new conservatives recognize that there must be an inward spiritual change before apologetics can have much value. Ellul echoes the views of several of the new breed: "As long as the human heart has not been transformed by

3 Karl Barth, *Church Dogmatics*, I, 1. Trans. G. T. Thomson (Edinburgh: T. & T. Clark, 1949), p. 31.

the Holy Spirit, it is impossible for one to be convinced of God's excellence, either by experience or by reason."[4]

While many neo-orthodox theologians were prone to separate Christian faith and metaphysics, contending that Christianity is not so much a view of the world as a report of the saving acts of God, the new evangelicals tend to hold that faith has profound metaphysical implications that must be worked out in opposition to cultural philosophy. They would point to the New Testament depiction of the depravity of man and the transient character of the world as their basis for asserting that Christianity entails a world-perspective of its own that stands in judgment over all purely cultural world views. It is well to note that in his *Theological Science* Thomas Torrance, who stands in the Barthian tradition, calls for theology to discover and develop its own metaphysical stance.

Weaknesses in the New Evangelicalism

Since the new evangelicalism is a mood and not a theological system, it is perhaps premature to point to doctrinal gaps or weaknesses. Yet it can be said that the doctrines of the church and the sacraments are conspicuously lacking in much contemporary evangelical writing. The "Protestant principle" needs to be united with "catholic substance" if the church is to maintain continuity with the worldwide apostolic tradition. In some of the recently established Protestant religious communities in Europe such as the Evangelical Sisterhood of Mary and the Brotherhood of Christ, both of which come out of evangelical revivals, a churchly and sacramental orientation is held in balance with personal faith and missionary enthusiasm.

Again, in an effort to make intelligible the funda-

4 Jacques Ellul, *The Meaning of the City* (Grand Rapids: Eerdmans, 1970), p. 40.

mentals of the faith, the temptation to construct an air-tight rational system is very alluring. The new evangelical theologians have thus far resisted this temptation, but we are now in a new theological climate and voices from the left (Pannenberg) as well as from the right (Gordon Clark) are calling for a renewed Christian rationalism. If evangelicalism is to remain true to its great heritage of Puritanism and Pietism, as well as the Reformation, it must not lose sight of the mystical or suprarational dimensions of the Christian faith.

An emphasis on the spiritual mission of the church should not blind us to the fact that social reforms must sometimes precede the preaching of the gospel. Ellul is one who disputes the idea that social action can be a means to the confrontation with the ultimate concern, but we must not forget that in the New Testament itself Jesus fed the hungry so that the people might perceive their spiritual hunger (Jn. 6), and He did miracles of healing so that men might be drawn closer to God. His motivation was love, but his goal was the conversion of souls. The great commission has theological priority over social service and political action but not always chrono-logical priority.

The social concern of the new evangelicals is one of the areas in which they diverge from popular fundamental-ism. Carl Henry has recently declared: "Fundamentalism has too long identified itself with status quo capitalism" and "must let the world feel the sting of a Christian alternative" to the social and political ills that now afflict us.[5] Leighton Ford has said that evangelical Christians have too long followed a culture-Christ—"a Jesus who wears red, white and blue."

Freedom from ideological and class interests is very necessary if any church or theology is to preserve the prophetic dimension of the Christian faith. In the recent past evangelicalism has become too closely dependent

[5] *Christian Herald,* Vol. XCIV, No. 5 (May, 1971), p. 8.

upon the bourgeois class, and it needs to rise above this dependence if it is to recover the radicalism that characterized its early history. At the same time it must not allow itself to become identified with other ideological positions—such as the New Left. Neo-orthodoxy, though it sounded warnings against the excesses of capitalism and the dangers of fascism, sometimes accepted uncritically the ideals and values of democratic socialism. This perhaps accounts for the fascination of many of those who have come out of neo-orthodoxy with the Christian-Marxist dialogue.

The relative dearth of devotional writing in the new evangelicalism is also a sign that this movement needs deeper theological and biblical grounding if it is to make a lasting impact on the modern church. The periods in which Puritanism and Pietism were dominant witnessed an outpouring of devotional literature—manuals of devotion, prayer guides and hymnology. It is true that today in conservative evangelical circles earlier devotional works (e.g., those by John Bunyan, John and Charles Wesley, Richard Baxter, Tersteegen, etc.) are being republished and circulated, but the strength of a movement lies in its ability to make an original and fresh contribution. Some progress is being made in this direction (e.g., Ellul's *Prayer and Modern Man,* Trueblood's *Confronting Christ,* Mackay's *His Life and Our Life,* Lindsell's *When You Pray* and Schaeffer's *True Spirituality*), but much work remains to be done.[6]

Finally we need to note the ambivalent position of the new evangelicalism toward ecumenism. Not only conservative theologians like Carl Henry and Harold Lindsell, but also such men as Jacques Ellul and John MacKay, who have worked within the conciliar movement, have voiced reservations about its desirability and efficacy. Mackay rightly laments the fact that whereas in its earlier

[6] In this connection I should also mention Robert Laaser, *Lessons Not Learned in School* (St. Louis: Eden Publishing House, 1972) and my own book *The Crisis of Piety* (Grand Rapids: Eerdmans, 1968).

years structure was made to serve the mission of the
church, now the concern for institutional consolidation
and organic mergers seems to predominate. Neither
Mackay nor Ellul opposes the principle of ecumenism,
but these men desire that it be biblically grounded and
turned in an evangelical direction, a concern that we
share.

Nevertheless evangelicals both within and without the
conciliar churches need to press their position within the
ecumenical councils if the ecumenical movement is to be
anchored once again in the biblical mandate of mission
and evangelism. If they choose to withdraw from or
remain outside the discussions, then they may, in Carl
Henry's words, become "a wilderness sect" instead of a
vanguard in the army of the Lord.

Some of the new evangelicals are now using the term
"evangelical ecumenism" in order to distinguish it from
conciliar ecumenism. Evangelical ecumenism aims for the
reconciliation of the various churches and the separated
brethren but not necessarily organic union. It sees dialogue not as a means to arrive at the truth but to clarify
and illumine the truth. It regards conversations with
Marxists and other religions as a means of furthering the
proclamation of the gospel instead of forging a new
cultural synthesis in which the Christian message would
be drastically diluted.

Prognosis

The question is being increasingly raised as to which
theological movement will be the successor to neo-
orthodoxy. In the forties and fifties neo-orthodoxy
formed the theological establishment, but its demise was
reflected in the rise of secular-radical theology in the
sixties. In addition to secular theology a neo-liberal movement has arisen that seeks to ground Christian faith in a
new kind of metaphysics. Can the latest brand of evangelicalism muster sufficient moral and intellectual re-

sources to challenge the new wave of modernism and liberalism? Will the new evangelicalism be seen by theological students of tomorrow as a living option and will it consequently become the successor of neo-orthodoxy? Only time will tell, but it is interesting to note that Dr. Elton Trueblood, who came out of an evangelical liberal tradition, now sees the new evangelicalism as a viable alternative to the new liberalism and radicalism.[7]

Like secular-radical theology and unlike dispensational fundamentalism and neo-orthodoxy, the new evangelical theology is basically optimistic. Yet its optimism does not reside in the inherent moral possibilities within man but in the reality of the corporeal resurrection of Jesus Christ and in the mystery of supernatural regeneration. It is characterized by a holy rather than a this-worldly optimism. But this is not to be confused with any kind of perfectionism, since it recognizes the persistence of sinful ambiguity even in godly persons. The new world that it looks to is the new heaven-earth ushered in by Jesus Christ, not a this-worldly utopian brotherhood of nations. Yet it does maintain that the victorious life can begin here and now, that the ideal of sainthood can be partially realized in the historical present. This is the kind of optimism that might find a hearing among a disillusioned and despairing generation.

It can be said that whereas neo-orthodoxy stressed spiritual alienation and secular theology the social revolution, the new evangelicalism places the accent on spiritual rebirth. But an effort is made to relate the inward change of heart to the social situation. Individual conversion is the precondition for revolutionary social change, and yet conversion by itself is not sufficient to effect such change. It must be supplemented by concerned social involvement but one that avoids all forms of utopianism.

Because the new evangelicalism is only in the embryo

[7] See Elton Trueblood, *The Future of the Christian* (N.Y.: Harper, 1971), pp. 61-82.

stage, because it does not constitute a unified pattern or school of theology, it is perhaps not yet able to forge a fresh, viable theological alternative. At the same time its flexibility and open-ended character augur well for the struggle that is coming.

The new conservative movement could break apart in several different directions. Streams of thought that are now converging might very well diverge in the future. The tension that existed in conservative Protestantism in the seventeenth and eighteenth centuries between Pietism and Orthodoxy is also present in the new evangelicalism. Some circles emphasize life and experience over doctrine and are tempted to go the way of spiritualism. (This is the bane of the charismatic movement.) Others are preoccupied with right doctrine and are vulnerable to the temptation to restore the old confessionalism. Still others who are alarmed at the excesses of higher biblical criticism might be propelled in the direction of a rigid biblicism, a new fundamentalism.

Evangelicals today must strive to be both radical and conservative. They must seek to go to the roots of the original faith and recover what is abiding and fundamental. They must not be content with accepting the values and clichés of any particular theological tradition, even of the evangelical Protestant tradition, but they must be bold enough to subject all traditions to the scrutiny of the original gospel message. At the same time they must seek to conserve the authentic spiritual values in all theological traditions, and particularly their own, even if these values are not explicitly written out in Scripture. But they must resolutely resist the way of reaction and repristination, for this road leads to obscurantism and fanaticism.

Moreover, a renewed evangelicalism must not hesitate to apply the gospel to the whole of life, to the political and economic as well as the private, personal spheres. The rampant individualism of a dying bourgeois culture, which was characterized by a privatism in morals, must be totally transcended if evangelicalism is to be a free and vital spiritual force in the new world.

The impending struggle between evangelicalism and liberalism can be likened to that between Puritans and traditionalist Anglicans in the seventeenth century and also to that between Pietists and Lutheran and Reformed confessionalists in the eighteenth century. It also bears a marked resemblance to the conflict between evangelical revivalism and the high church and liberal Anglicans in eighteenth- and nineteenth-century England.

The battle must be waged on two fronts. Evangelicals must beware of the dangers on the radical right as well as on the left. A rigid, confessional orthodoxy is as apt to quench and grieve the Spirit as an attenuated liberalism. But the truth must not be sought in the golden mean between extremes, in the way of moderation, for this too is alien to the faith of the gospel. Charles Simeon, Anglican evangelical in the nineteenth century, boldly remarked that the truth lies in both extremes, and we are therefore compelled to stand sometimes on the right and sometimes on the left in order to hold onto the paradoxes and mysteries of the faith.

The theological future may well belong to a chastened and resurgent evangelicalism, but much work remains if the vision of a catholic and evangelical church is to be realized. Where the Holy Spirit is active, demonic forces are also at work, and the strength of this new movement will lie in its ability to discern the spirits, to separate the wheat of the gospel from the chaff of human speculation. Only time will tell whether the new evangelicalism will prove to be a formidable theological option in the remaining part of the twentieth century.

III

The Hallmarks of Evangelicalism

Evangelicalism has various meanings, and some of these are ambiguous. Its root meaning is to be found in the New Testament word *evangelion*, referring to evangel or gospel. It is right to say that its basic connotation is theological. It concerns the message of the New Testament church regarding salvation through the cross and resurrection of Jesus Christ. To be evangelical means to believe that we are justified only by grace through faith in Him who suffered and died for our sins. "Evangelical" also refers to the spirit in which this message is proclaimed, the spirit of zeal and earnestness. In addition this word has a historical meaning, since it is associated with a spiritual movement of renewal within Protestantism after the Reformation. In the context of this chapter the theological meaning will be normative.

It should not be overlooked that evangelicalism has been present in Roman Catholicism as well as in Protestantism. The Second Council of Orange (529) definitely reflected an evangelical stance: "Our salvation requires that we assert and believe that, in every good work we do, it is not we who have the initiative, aided subsequently by the mercy of God, but that he begins by inspiring faith and love towards him, without any prior merit of ours . . ." (Canon 25). St. Augustine, who is claimed by both Catholics and evangelical Protestants, was staunch in his defense of the divine authority of Scripture, justification by grace alone and the sole efficacy of the atoning merits of Jesus Christ. He declared: "The righteousness of the saints in this world consists more in the forgiveness of sins than in the perfection of virtues." Other theologians within Roman Catholicism in whom evangelical piety can be perceived at least to some degree are Bernard of Clairvaux, Thomas Aquinas, John Tauler, John of the Cross, Teresa of Avila and Pascal, and, of course, this list could be greatly expanded. In our own day we might mention Hans Küng, Ida Frederieke Görres, Louis Bouyer, Josef Geiselmann and Raymond Brown.

At the same time philosophical elements drawn from both Platonism and Aristotelianism infiltrated Roman Catholic as well as Eastern Orthodox thinking and piety, and the biblical message of salvation by grace was compromised by a view that ascetical exercises can prepare the way for the reception of grace. A mystical conception of love as Eros obscured the biblical doctrine of Agape, the love that does not seek its own. Anders Nygren in his monumental work *Agape and Eros* contends that this mystical notion became dominant even in such luminaries as Augustine and Aquinas. In the later middle ages a synergistic orientation came to prevail in which justification was attributed to works of love in addition to faith.[1]

The Protestant Reformation signalized the recovery of the biblical and authentically catholic message that we are justified by grace alone through faith. Our salvation lies only in the merits of Christ and not in man's innate capacity to earn the grace of justification. The Reformers also held to the sovereign authority of Scripture—over experience and over the church. They did not wish to discard the catholic wisdom of the past but to appraise this wisdom in the light of God's holy Word. They sought an evangelical catholicism—one that stands in continuity

---

[1] See Philip Watson, *Let God Be God* (London: Epworth, 1948), pp. 48-65.

with the church tradition as well as one based on the
authority of Scripture.

At the same time it cannot be denied that because of
the controversy of the age the Reformers underplayed
certain emphases that also have their basis in the Bible.
This is even more true for some of the orthodox heirs of
the Reformation. The life of holiness and the need for
spiritual disciplines, though still stressed by Luther and
Calvin, were pushed very much into the background in
the circles of Protestant orthodoxy. In their antipathy to
legalism or works-righteousness the practical side of the
Christian life came to be regarded as of lesser importance
than creedal statements defending the faith of the Reformation. In reaction to a barren confessionalism spiritual
movements of purification emerged—Pietism, Puritanism
and Evangelicalism—all of which sought to incorporate
the catholic stress on the holy life into a theology of free
grace. These movements may be regarded as a new flowering of evangelicalism subsequent to the Reformation,
though they in turn often succumbed to the temptations
of legalism and perfectionism. In the twentieth century
evangelicalism has been represented in fundamentalism,
the theology of crisis (neo-orthodoxy) and neo-evangelicalism. None of these movements has succeeded in recov-
ering the treasures of our catholic heritage in addition to
the biblical message of free grace, and perhaps this task
still lies before us. This is to say that the original intention of the Reformers to create a Reformed catholicism
remains unfulfilled.

Evangelicals, of course, should not regard themselves as
the only Christians. Because of their special emphases
they can be put in a class by themselves, and yet this very
separation from other Christians makes them more vulnerable to sectarianism and pharisaism. One should be
reminded that evangelicals hold much in common with
other orthodox Christians. Among doctrines and affirmations that can be considered orthodox and biblical but
not uniquely evangelical are the following: the ontologi-

cal trinity; the incarnation of Christ; His Virgin Birth; His bodily resurrection; the reality of the supernatural, including miracles; the church as the body of Christ; the sacraments as effectual signs or means of grace; personal immortality; and the final resurrection. Other doctrines could also be mentioned, and one cannot be truly or fully evangelical apart from an assent to these truths of revelation.

Too often, especially in the recent past, evangelicals have played down the mystical and sacramental aspects of the faith out of a bias against Roman Catholicism. But an evangelicalism divorced from the mystical and sacramental tradition of Catholicism succumbs to a biblical rationalism and sometimes ugly sectarianism.

Evangelicalism stands in continuity with orthodoxy, but it should forever beware of orthodoxism, where faith becomes characterized as assent to dogma. It should seek to be confessional but should eschew all forms of creedalism in which church authority is given priority over the Bible. A true evangelical will be fundamental in his beliefs, but he will try to avoid the kind of hyper-fundamentalism that practically deifies the Scriptures. He will see the rightful place for the historical-critical method, though he will remember with Peter Forsyth that criticism cannot give us the Word of God. He will be conservative in that he will seek to preserve the values of the ecclesiastical tradition, but he will not be reactionary in that he will not wish simply to return to the past. He will differentiate the faith once delivered to the saints from the "old-time religion" that characterizes a particular historical period in the past. He will be radical in the sense of going to the roots of the faith, but he will not be ideological, trying to unite the faith with a social or political philosophy. It is interesting to note that the early issues of the evangelical-holiness magazine *The Gospel Trumpet* (Church of God, Anderson, Indiana) carried the following descriptive slogan in its masthead: "A Definite, Radical, Non-Sectarian Journal." This indeed mir-

rors the evangelical ideal, though in popular evangelicalism the radical and catholic dimensions of the faith have
often been forfeited in the interests of self-preservation
and cultural respectability.

The Sovereignty of God

If there is anything that characterizes the evangelical
and Reformed tradition it is the stress upon the sovereignty of God. Not a philosophical abstraction, whether
this be called the ground of being, the world soul, or the
creative event, but the living God of the Bible who is
sovereign over heaven and earth—this is the God of evangelicalism. He is the One referred to as "God the Almighty" (Gen. 17:1; Rev. 21:22) and is alone deserving
of worship and reverence. But to affirm the omnipotence
of God does not mean to confound this with arbitrary or
unrestricted power, for this too is a philosophical conception. The omnipotence of God means that He is a God of
conquering love. He is not inherently dependent on man,
but He makes Himself dependent out of compassion for
the sinner. He can and does answer our every request
made in the name of Jesus Christ, but He will answer in
His own way and time.

To hold to the sovereignty of God in the biblical sense
means also to affirm His transcendence. "Heaven and the
highest heaven" cannot contain Him (I Kings 8:27). But
He is not transcendent as the deists understand this, for
He condescends to our level in the person of Jesus Christ.
He is not only transcendent but also immanent as indwelling Spirit. Although He comes to us He never becomes a part of us. Although He is the center of our
being, He is not accessible to us except as He makes
Himself accessible. The sovereign God of the Bible is
enveloped in mystery and therefore must be approached
in awe and reverence.

Sovereignty also connotes freedom. God is not bound
to the world, though He identifies Himself with the

suffering and travail of His people. Neither is He bound to human law and logic, though He makes His Word available to us in human modes of expression. His is a freedom in love. He is not characterized by the freedom to act capriciously, but rather He acts responsibly in self-giving love. He is not arbitrary in His judgments but faithful to His inner will and being.

This God is both a God of holiness and a God of love. His holiness or wrath is, however, one form of His love. His love can be so merciful that it appears devoid of mercy. He is angry with His people because of His love, and He disciplines and chastises them out of His concern for their welfare. Holiness signifies an intolerance of sin though not a rejection of the sinner. It signifies a demand for purity but not as the basis for man's justification or acceptance by God.

Sovereignty in the biblical sense likewise entails omniscience. God knows the course of the future and the fulfillment of the future, but this must not be taken to mean that He literally knows every single event even before it happens. It means that He knows every alternative and the way in which His children may well respond to the decisions that confront them. The plan of God is predetermined, but the way in which He realizes it is dependent partly on the free cooperation of His subjects. This does not detract from His omnipotence, for it means that He is so powerful that He is willing to attain His objectives by allowing a certain room for freedom of action on the part of man.

H. Richard Niebuhr has reminded us in his *The Kingdom of God in America* that it is not the vision of God (as in Catholic mysticism) but the sovereignty of God that has been the principal motif in evangelical religion. The accent is thereby placed not on contemplation but on spiritual and ethical obedience, in seeking to bring our wills into conformity with His will.

The motto of the Reformation, particularly the Calvinistic side, was *soli Deo gloria*, glory to God alone.

Calvin declared: "Surely the first foundation of righteousness is the worship of God. When this is overthrown, all the remaining parts of righteousness, like the pieces of a shattered and fallen building, are mangled and scattered."[2] The glory of God, for Calvin, is the foundation for active obedience and service to our neighbor. In his oft-quoted words:

> We are not our own: in so far as we can, let us therefore forget ourselves and all that is ours. Conversely, we are God's: let us therefore live for him and die for him. We are God's: let all the parts of our life accordingly strive toward him as our only lawful goal.[3]

Evangelical theology is both theocentric and Christocentric. It opposes a syncretistic mysticism whereby God is depicted as an impersonal ground of being or as the undifferentiated unity. It also stands against an evolutionary naturalism in which God is conceived as a vital force in nature or as a creative process in the world. The God of biblical faith is the very opposite of that described by Kazantzakis, a modern evolutionary naturalist: "Our God is not almighty, he is not all-holy, he is not certain that he will conquer, he is not certain that he will be conquered."[4]

Evangelicalism upholds the sovereign Creator-God of the Bible as over against the finite god of process philosophy and liberal theology. It also opposes the impassible, static God of Hellenistic philosophy which intruded time and again into orthodox theology. The true God is not an impersonal ground of unity or world soul but active and dynamic will. He is the living Lord of history rather than a self-contained, timeless absolute. He is the "personal-

---

[2] John Calvin, *Institutes of the Christian Religion.* Ed. John T. McNeill. Trans. Ford Lewis Battles (Philadelphia: Westminster, 1960), II, 8, 11, p. 377.

[3] *Ibid.*, III, 7, 1, p. 690.

[4] Nikos Kazantzakis, *The Saviors of God.* Trans. Kimon Friar (N.Y.: Simon & Schuster, 1960), p. 116.

infinite God" (Francis Schaeffer) rather than an eternal principle or transcendent ideal. The choice today as in much of the past is between the living all-powerful God of biblical, evangelical religion on the one hand and the abstractions of cultural philosophy and the sentimental, permissive gods of culture-religion on the other.

The Divine Authority of Scripture

Evangelical theology appeals to Scripture as the infallible norm for faith and practice. Holy Scripture is the inspired record of God's revelation and its divinely appointed medium. The apostle proclaimed: "All scripture is inspired by God and profitable for teaching, for reproof, for correction, and for training in righteousness, that the man of God may be complete, equipped for every good work" (II Tim. 3:16, 17). We are also told that the apostles speak in words that the Holy Ghost teaches (I Cor. 2:13). Inspiration means that the Scriptures have God as their primary author even though they are also the product of men who lived in a particular time and place.

The divine inspiration of Scripture has sometimes been interpreted as signifying a mechanical dictation so that the writers are simply passive pens of the Holy Spirit. But the main body of evangelicalism, including the Reformation, has recognized that the writers are real authors and that the words and imagery that they employ therefore bear the stamp of cultural relativity. But it is in and through these culturally conditioned words that God speaks His eternal, unconditional Word. The Scriptures present to us the Word of God in the concrete speech of a particular people, in what Barth calls "the language of Canaan."

Inspiration conveys the truth that the writers were guided in their selection of words and meanings so that their overall witness is reliable and trustworthy. By virtue of its divine inspiration, the Bible can be regarded as an adequate and normative expression of God's will and purpose. Yet its manner of expression often shows the taint of human weakness and infirmity (Bavinck). Calvin said that the Holy Spirit accommodated Himself to the cultural milieu and historical limitations of the writers. The truth of revelation did not drop from heaven but was discovered in significant encounters and occurrences, in the crises and trials that confronted the people of Israel. The eyes of the prophets and apostles were opened by the Spirit of God to the divine significance of the crucial events of their times.

Scripture has a divine but at the same time a derivative authority. The Bible is authoritative because it is centered in Jesus Christ and conveys the truth about Christ. The ultimate authority lies in God Himself and His Son. Jesus said: "All authority in heaven and on earth has been given to me" (Mt. 28:18). The Bible's authority is dependent on Jesus Christ, and it is His Spirit that guarantees the trustworthiness of its witness. Calvin maintained that "the highest proof of Scripture derives . . . from the fact that God in person speaks in it."[5]

When it is said that Scripture is the infallible rule for faith and practice, this must be taken to mean the Bible as a whole and interpreted by the Spirit. Any text when not seen in its spiritual and theological context becomes an occasion for misunderstanding and deception.[6] When evangelical theology affirms that Scripture does not err, it means that whatever Christ teaches in Scripture is completely true. Scripture is without error in its matter, i.e., in its basic teaching and witness.[7] But this heavenly doctrine or teaching is not self-evident and can only be

[5] John Calvin, *Institutes*, I, 7, 4, p. 78.

[6] The Second Helvetic Confession went so far as to maintain that the letter divorced from the Spirit "works wrath and provokes sin" in the minds of those who do not have the Spirit (ch. XIII).

[7] And we must hasten to add that this includes not only its testimony concerning God and salvation, but also its interpretation of man, life and history. But this does not imply perfect factual accuracy in all details as the extreme literalist holds.

discovered by wrestling with Scripture under the guidance and illumination of the Holy Spirit.

It can be said that Scripture *is* the Word of God and also contains the Word of God. It is both a human witness to God, to His purpose and dealings with man, and God's testimony concerning Himself. But this unity or identity between the human witness and the divine revelation is an indirect one. The Word of God is not the letter or text by itself but the divine meaning imbedded in the text, a meaning unveiled only by the Holy Spirit (cf. II Cor. 3:6). The Spirit of God reveals what He intended to teach the biblical author and what the author faintly grasped (cf. Ps. 139:6; I Pet. 1:10, 11) and what He intends to teach us today through the author's broken but faithful witness. A. W. Tozer of the Christian and Missionary Alliance criticizes the hyper-fundamentalist view that says, "If you learn the text you've got the truth. . . . Such see no beyond and no mystic depth, no mysterious heights, nothing supernatural or divine."[8]

An authentic evangelical theology will also affirm that biblical authority does not imply a narrow biblical literalism. We should begin with the literal or natural meaning of the text but then seek to relate it to its wider spiritual context. If the Holy Spirit intended that the writer's words be understood symbolically, it is manifestly unbiblical to treat them otherwise. An excessive biblical literalism may lead to a rigid dispensationalism in which the spiritual kingdom of Christ is confused with a this-worldly Jewish millennial kingdom.

Nor does evangelical theology deny the rightful place for the historical criticism of Scripture, though it sees criticism as having a limited role. The historical-critical method can throw light upon the cultural and historical background of the text, but it cannot lay hold of the divine significance of the text. It can uncover the then current meanings of the biblical words, but it cannot

[8] Gerald B. Smith, ed., *The Tozer Pulpit,* Vol. III (Harrisburg, Pa.: Christian Publications, 1970), pp. 13, 14.

bring us the Word of God. The principle of historical criticism is valid, since Scripture is the word of man as well as the Word of God.

The motto of all theology that claims to be evangelical is *sola scriptura* (Scripture alone). This should not be taken to mean that Scripture is the only source of revelation but that it is the original historical source of revelation; God Himself is, of course, the ultimate source of His revelation. Moreover, Scripture is the criterion or standard for all continuing revelation. This means that religious experience must be tested in the light of Scripture and not vice versa.

Sola scriptura also means that Scripture interprets itself by the working of the Holy Spirit. We can say too that the Spirit is the interpreter of Scripture, but what He gives us is that which is already contained in Scripture, even if only implicitly. The church is a servant of the Spirit in its interpretation of the Bible. The Bible needs to be expounded by the church, but the church must always stand under the Bible in its proclamation and interpretation.

The Protestant Reformers were adamant that the ecclesiastical tradition, while containing much spiritual wisdom, should never be placed on a par with Scripture. The tradition must instead be corrected and judged by the Scriptures. Calvin exclaimed: "But a most pernicious error widely prevails that Scripture has only so much weight as is conceded to it by the consent of the church. As if the eternal and inviolable truth of God depended upon the decision of men!"[9]

Evangelicals contend against the neo-Protestants that the Word made flesh must never be divorced from the Word expressed in Scripture. The divine wisdom incarnate and the divine wisdom inscribed are correlative. Christ is the content of Scripture, and Scripture is the cradle in which Christ is laid (Luther). The divine treasure

[9] John Calvin, *Institutes*, I, 7, 1, p. 75.

is available to us only in this earthen vessel, the Holy
Bible.

Total Depravity

Evangelicalism holds to the total depravity of man
against the Enlightenment doctrine of man's fundamental
goodness. As it is stated in Psalm 51:5: "Behold, I was
brought forth in iniquity, and in sin did my mother
conceive me." We are not simply born into a sinful world
but we are born as sinners or as persons inwardly propelled toward sin.

The doctrine of total depravity does not mean that
there is no goodness in human nature but that all of our
goodness is corrupted by sin. It means that no dimension
of our being is free from the taint of sin, whether this be
reason, will or feeling. Our original or essential nature has
been created good, but our present, existential nature is
corrupt. And this corruption has its seat in the very
center of our being. Jeremiah confessed: "The heart is
deceitful above all things, and desperately corrupt; who
can understand it?" (Jer. 17:9).

Sin is not the loss of a supernatural endowment (as in
Thomism) nor an inherent weakness or ignorance (as in
Protestant liberalism). It does not consist in mere deficiency or privation but in positive rebellion and perver-
sity. It entails bondage to powers or forces beyond our
control and also blindness in the area of morality and
religion. Augustine described it as a perversion of the will,
a perversion that affects the direction of man's reasoning
as well as his powers of discernment.

Catholic theology has traditionally made a distinction
between the tinder of sin and the act of sin. The Reformers rightly perceived that both of these should be
regarded as sin. Indeed, before the act of sin there exists a
propensity to sin which is within us from birth. Through
the grace of God man can withstand this evil inclination,
but it is never wholly destroyed until the state of glory.

This is to say that man, even the Christian, is always vulnerable to temptation, though by the power of the indwelling Spirit he can lead a life victorious over sin.

The deepest meaning of sin is that it is a disease or contagion. The liability to this disease is inherent in the human condition. This sinful bias is passed on through human inheritance, though it is not a part of our created being. It is not a physical taint but a spiritual infection, one that has penetrated our biological nature and is transmitted by human generation.

This means that man can be saved only by God's grace, since he is unable and unwilling to save himself. Our free will is in servitude to sin; though we continue to be free from necessity, we are not free from sin. Total depravity means that apart from God's grace we find ourselves in total bondage. But the chains that hold us in captivity can be broken by the Spirit of God through faith in Jesus Christ.

The root of sin is unbelief, and its prime manifestations are pride, sensuality and fear. Sin is not simply concupiscence or lust but the lust for power. It is not mere weakness but wickedness.

Salvation dawns upon us when we are awakened to our sin and seek the help and comfort of the holy God. It is only when we cease relying on ourselves and place our trust in Jesus Christ that we become free from the dominion of sin. When one enters into this freedom, however, he is constrained to confess that he is "only a sinner saved by grace."

The Substitutionary Atonement

The heart of the gospel is that Jesus Christ died in our place by His sacrifice on the cross. By His death and resurrection He has delivered us from the powers of this world—sin, death and the devil. We deserve to die because of our sins, but God took upon Himself the penalty of our sin by tasting suffering and death in the person of His

Son. The death of Christ was redemptive because it atoned for our sins.

This is why evangelical theology affirms with the apostle: "In him we have redemption through his blood, the forgiveness of our trespasses, according to the riches of his grace" (Eph. 1:7). And also: "Without the shedding of blood there is no forgiveness of sins" (Heb. 9:22; cf. I Jn. 1:7).

The atonement of Christ at Calvary has been interpreted in orthodox theology as both a ransom for our sins and as a satisfaction for sin. These are not at variance, for they convey the double truth that Christ's death was both a ransom to the powers of darkness and the satisfaction of the justice of God. Though it spelled defeat by the powers of the world, it also signified a royal victory, for in rising from the grave Christ triumphed over death, Satan and hell. The drama of the cross and resurrection was not only a revelation of divine love but also a demonstration of divine power.

Evangelical theology has always insisted that the atonement has two poles: the objective sacrifice on the cross and the subjective appropriation of the benefits of this sacrifice in faith. The truth in the moral influence and mystical theories of the atonement is that man must make contact with the cross of Christ if he is to benefit from its saving power.

Though Christ's agonizing death for sin is finished and cannot be repeated or renewed (cf. Jn. 19:30; Heb. 9:25-28), his suffering for the salvation of men continues in His role as Intercessor. Christ revealed to Paul that he felt the persecution against His people, and Hebrews 6:6 speaks of apostates crucifying the Son of God anew and putting him to open shame. Paul wrote that Christ will not rest content "until he has put all his enemies under his feet" (I Cor. 15:25). Pascal also affirmed the continuing passion of Christ: "Jesus shall be in agony until the end of the world." Though this theme was not a dominant one in the theology of the Reformers, it is certainly present in these words of Luther: "When we suffer and die, we should bravely believe and be certain that not we or we alone, but Christ and the church suffers and dies with us."

To affirm the substitutionary atonement does not imply that the Christian is thereby exempt from suffering. Only the suffering of Christ atones for sin, but the disciple of Christ must suffer in bearing witness to his Savior. He is called to take up the cross and follow his Lord in a life of costly discipleship. He cannot make reparation for the sins of others, but he can and should bear the burdens of others (Gal. 6:2).

Our suffering does not atone for sin, but it is a witness and sign of the atonement at Calvary. It is also a channel or instrument whereby men are brought into contact with the cross of Christ. To affirm the vicarious, substitutionary atonement of Christ without identifying ourselves with the sufferings and needs of others is to make a mockery of our salvation. Free grace thereby becomes cheap grace, and this was a temptation even at the time of the Reformation. Luther warned against this peril:

> Astounding it is that the cross of Christ has so fallen into forgetfulness, for is it not forgetfulness of the cross when no one wishes to suffer but rather to enjoy himself and evade the cross? You must personally experience suffering with Christ. He suffered for your sake and should you not suffer for his sake, as well as for your own?[10]

Salvation by Grace

Certainly another hallmark of an evangelical, biblical theology is *sola gratia*, salvation by divine grace. As it is written: "He saved us, not because of deeds done by us in righteousness, but in virtue of his own mercy" (Tit. 3:5; cf. Dan. 9:18). Not by works of penance or deeds of

---

[10] Roland Bainton, ed. and trans., *Luther's Meditations on the Gospels* (Philadelphia: Westminster, 1962), p. 136.

mercy but by divine compassion are sinners justified and delivered.

Paul maintained that we are pardoned even while we are still in our sins (Rom. 5:8). The divine justification is not conditional upon anything that we can do or merit. It must be received by faith, but faith is not a work of man but a work of the Spirit of God within us. We are made active by faith, but the fruits that we bear in a life of faithfulness confirm and attest but do not earn the grace of justification.

Scripture tells us that we are not only pardoned by grace but also cleansed by grace. Christ not only forgives sin; He also takes away sin. The saving work of Christ entails regeneration and sanctification as well as justification. But this inward renewing and cleansing is a lifelong process. It has a definite beginning, but it must continue while we are still in this mortal flesh. According to Luther, "This work of renewal and purification is not completed all at once, but He daily labors with us and purifies us so that we become continuously purer and purer."[11]

Evangelical theology is noted for its claim that grace does not merely aid the will of man but transforms him. Our free will does not need to be assisted but converted. It is not enough for human nature to be repaired; it must be drastically changed. Indeed, man stands in need of a new nature, a new heart, new hopes and aspirations. The stony heart must be replaced by a "heart of flesh" (cf. Ezek. 11:19; II Cor. 5:17; Eph. 4:22-24).

Evangelical theology affirms against all kinds of Pelagianism and synergism that we are saved not by free will but by free grace. Augustine declared: "Liberty comes by grace, and not grace by liberty." This does not mean that man lacks a free will but only that his free will does not in any way procure his salvation. Bernard of Clairvaux,

[11] *Dr. Martin Luther's Sammtliche Werke*, 8 Band (Erlangen: Verlag von Carl Hender, 1827), p. 175.

who inspired Arminius as well as Luther and Calvin, put it this way:

> Take away free will, and nothing will be left to be saved. Take away grace, and nothing will be left as the source of salvation. This work cannot be effected without two parties—one, from whom it may come: the other, to whom or in whom it may be wrought. God is the author of salvation. Free will only is capable of being saved (from his *De libero arbitrio et gratia*).

Instead of exalting free will evangelical theology is much more inclined to uphold a liberated will, a will that is set free for service and discipleship. When man's will is liberated from its bondage to sin, then man is free to cooperate with God in the service of His kingdom. He does not cooperate in the obtaining of the remission of sins, but he is made a covenant-partner of God in the advancement of His kingdom.

Sola gratia means that man's hope lies not in a reformation of character but in a regeneration of being. Man must be born anew from above (Jn. 3:3-6). The conversion of the heart takes precedence over the education of the mind. The apostolic mission has priority over works of social service.

The doctrine of salvation by grace is the basis for a holy optimism. We do not need to make ourselves acceptable to God before we can receive His forgiveness. We need only confess our unworthiness and helplessness. God forgives us while we are still sinners, but this is not the end of the story. God does not leave us in our sins but instead sends His Holy Spirit to us to renew and empower us for service in His kingdom. Calvary must be fulfilled in Pentecost if we are to receive the full salvation that Christ promises. We are not only saved by grace but also empowered by grace and kept by grace. Those who rely not on their own powers but on divine grace will persevere to the end: this indeed is the truth in the Calvinist doctrine of the perseverance of the saints.

Faith Alone

Martin Luther came to an assurance of his salvation only when he was persuaded that man is justified by faith alone (*sola fide*) and not by good works. He declared: "Now the article of justification, which is our sole defence, not only against all the force and craft of men, but also against the gates of hell, is this: that by faith only in Christ, and without works, we are pronounced righteous and saved."[12] St. Paul made substantially the same affirmation: "For I am not ashamed of the gospel: it is the power of God for salvation to every one who has faith. . . . For man believes with his heart and so is justified, and he confesses with his lips and so is saved" (Rom. 1:16; 10:10; cf. 5:1).

The mainstream of the Roman Catholic tradition has also voiced this view, though this was not the general teaching at the time of the Reformation. It is well to note that the Augsburg Confession quotes approvingly from St. Ambrose in one of its articles on justification (Ch. VI): "It is ordained of God that whoever believes in Christ shall be saved, and he shall have forgiveness of sins, not through works but through faith alone, without merit."

Although our salvation is to be attributed to the grace of God alone, it must be received by faith if it is to benefit us. Yet faith itself is a gift of God, for we cannot believe until the Holy Spirit grants us the power and motivation. Both the awakening to faith and the repentance that follows signify that we are already recipients of divine grace.

Faith consists of knowledge, intellectual assent and trust (*fiducia*). The Reformers stressed the last aspect, but they did not exclude the cognitive dimensions of faith. Faith might be defined as the commitment of the

[12] Martin Luther, *A Commentary on St. Paul's Epistle to the Galatians*. Trans. Philip Watson (London: James Clarke, 1953), p. 218.

whole man to the living Christ, but this involves knowledge and assent.

Today in many circles faith is described as an irrational leap in the dark. But the New Testament understands it as walking in the light. One believes on the basis of evidence that faith itself provides—the assurance of forgiveness and the resurrection of Christ. At the same time this is evidence that is not available to sight or natural reason.

We are not only justified by faith alone, but we must also walk by faith alone, not by sight. We should not seek for evidential or rational signs that can buttress our faith. Jesus said that the kingdom of God is not coming with signs to be observed (Lk. 17:20). Calvin maintained that there is "nothing more injurious to faith than to fasten our minds to our eyes, that we may from what we see, seek a reason for our hope."[13]   And in the words of that great Catholic mystic John of the Cross: "Faith is . . . the only means whereby God manifests himself to the soul in his divine light, which surpasses all understanding."[14]

The awakening to faith is the new birth. We are not born into the kingdom of God, but we enter this kingdom in the decision of faith. Kierkegaard said that in baptism one is given a name, but in "the Moment of decision" he gives his name to Christianity. This often takes the form of a crisis experience, but even when this experience is not of the cataclysmic variety, it always marks a critical turning point in our lives. Oswald Chambers put it very succinctly: "The entrance into the kingdom is through the panging pains of repentance crashing into a man's respectable goodness."[15]

Evangelicals insist against sacramentalists that grace is

[13] John Calvin, *Commentaries on the Epistle of Paul the Apostle to the Romans*. Trans. John Owen (Edinburgh: Calvin Translation Society, 1849), p. 176.
[14] John of the Cross, *Ascent to Mount Carmel*, II, 9.
[15] Oswald Chambers, *My Utmost for His Highest* (London: Marshall, Morgan & Scott, 1967), p. 342.

not conferred automatically through outward ritual but that it must be appropriated in a personal commitment of faith. This is not to deny that the sacraments are indeed signs and means of grace, and this certainly includes baptism, even of infants, but we are not made Christians irrespective of our response to grace. We affirm the reality of baptismal grace in the rite of infant baptism, but unless this grace gives rise to faith, it does not guarantee or effect our salvation. Faith is both a fruit of baptismal or preparatory grace, and a response to it.

Primacy of Proclamation

Evangelicals stress the preaching and hearing of the Word of God over audio-visual aids, rituals and symbols, though this is not to deny the rightful place of these things. Preaching is considered the primary means of grace, but not any kind of preaching; the vehicle of God's Spirit is the preaching of the law and gospel—biblical, kerygmatic preaching. Paul affirmed: "So faith comes from what is heard, and what is heard comes by the preaching of Christ" (Rom. 10:17). And again: "For since, in the wisdom of God, the world did not know God through wisdom, it pleased God through the folly of what we preach to save those who believe" (I Cor. 1:21).

In their reaction against the Latin Mass in which preaching played an insignificant role the Protestant Reformers placed the emphasis upon the proclaimed Word of God. Luther declared: "For we must first hear the Word, and then afterwards the Holy Ghost works in our hearts; he works in the hearts of whom he will, and how he will, but never without the Word."[16] The Second Helvetic Confession of the Swiss Reformed Church calls the preaching of the Word of God the very Word of God. Preaching came to have the same function as absolution

[16] Martin Luther, *The Table Talk of Martin Luther*. Ed. Thomas Kepler (Cleveland: World, 1952), p. 143.

and confession in the Catholic church: the Word from the pulpit was seen as the keys that loose men from the shackles of sin. Preaching came to be a virtual sacrament in the churches of the Reformation.

Evangelical theology also insists that the written Word is a powerful means of grace. Indeed, the written Word is the basis for the proclaimed Word, just as the revealed Word, Jesus Christ, is the basis for the written Word. The church is subordinate to the Bible just as the Bible is subordinate to Jesus Christ and the gospel.

In the Reformed tradition we also speak of the visible Word—meaning here the sacraments. Yet the sacraments have never been seen as a means of grace apart from the Word written and proclaimed. This orientation can be seen today in the Catholic theologian Hans Küng: "The elements by themselves have no significance . . . it is in the light of the word that we should understand the Lord's Supper. The word here has not primarily the function of consecrating and transforming, but of proclaiming and testifying."[17]

Puritanism with its stress on the immediacy of the Word tended to dissociate God's presence from historical, ecclesiastical channels. Revivalistic Protestantism has always been in danger of seeking for truth in an inward experience instead of in the Word and sacraments. A catholic evangelicalism will never exalt experience over the Word but instead will look beyond immediate experience to the Word that is given to us in the sermon, the Bible and the sacraments.

The Christian life will likewise be seen as a means of grace, but only in conjunction with the Word. There is much talk today of witnessing by Christian presence, but Christian presence must always be based on and accompanied by the evangelical proclamation. Life and Word go together; while the former is the fruit the latter is the root or foundation.

17 Hans Küng, *The Church*. Trans. Ray and Rosaleen Ockenden (N.Y.: Sheed & Ward, 1967), p. 219.

Scriptural Holiness

Evangelical theology not only sounds the theme of justification by grace alone but also upholds the call to Scriptural holiness. The Anglican evangelical, Bishop Ryle, echoes the views of many: "We need the work of the Holy Spirit as well as the work of Christ; we need renewal of the heart as well as the atoning blood; we need to be sanctified as well as to be justified."[18]

While justification places man in a new relationship with God, sanctification makes him a new creation. In justification man is covered by the righteousness of God; in sanctification man is engrafted into this righteousness. Justification signifies a change in status, sanctification a change in being.

The work of the Holy Spirit brings man into conformity with Christ in a life of holiness. It is the Holy Spirit who effects regeneration and sanctification, inward cleansing and separation from sin. Man is made holy not by ascetic or mystical feats but by continual surrender to the Spirit of Christ in faith.

The Reformers were quick to uphold Christ as Savior, but they also made a real place for Christ as our Example. Luther criticized the piety of the imitation of Christ, but he stressed the necessity to follow Christ in a life of discipleship and thereby to become conformed to His image.

The evangelical movements after the Reformation were particularly insistent that personal holiness is as important as doctrinal orthodoxy. For Philip Spener, Richard Baxter, John Owen, John Wesley and many others the words in Hebrews 12:14 took on a new significance: "Strive . . . for the holiness without which no one will see the Lord." Wesley like the others was aware that our holiness does not entitle us to heaven; only the alien righteousness of Christ does that. Yet personal holiness

---

[18] J. C. Ryle, *Holiness* (Cambridge: James Clarke, 1956), p. 23.

qualifies us for heaven; it makes us ready and fit to enter the state of glory.

Evangelical theology holds that holiness in life is a fruit and evidence of justifying faith. Jonathan Edwards maintained that "Christian practice" is the evidential sign of our election. Personal holiness does not earn our salvation, but it confirms and attests a salvation already received in faith.

Scriptural holiness signifies a life of costly discipleship. It means bearing the cross in faith as a sign and witness of the salvation wrought by Christ at Calvary. Holiness entails a life of persevering faith and outgoing love. It means bearing the burdens of others out of gratefulness for what Christ has done for us. The cross that we bear strengthens our faith and equips us for service, but it does not atone for sin.

Holiness in life can be spoken of as "Christian perfection" in the sense of spiritual maturity. This indeed is our immediate goal as Christians in this life, but our ultimate goal is the absolute perfection of Jesus Christ. We cannot attain the very perfection of God while still in mortal flesh, but we can grow into a spiritual maturity that consists in wholeness, resoluteness, fidelity and love. Such maturity must not be confused with sinlessness or faultlessness. Sin is still present in the life of a Christian, but it no longer has dominion. Yet the powers of darkness seek to regain control and reestablish their rule. This is why the Christian is engaged in a lifelong struggle against sin, the flesh and the devil. The old man has been crucified in baptism and faith, but he continues to make trouble, even as a corpse coming back to life (Luther).

The life of the Christian is therefore one of penitence, since the consciousness of sin will drive him ever again to the cross of Christ for mercy and forgiveness. In the words of Luther: "When our Lord and Master, Jesus Christ, said 'Repent,' He called for the entire life of believers to be one of repentance."

At the same time the Christian life is also characterized

by victory through the power of the Holy Spirit. Though we are constantly vulnerable to temptation, we can be assured of overcoming every evil thought and desire by the grace of God. Moreover, we not only receive grace in faith but also grow in grace. The sanctifying work of the Holy Spirit makes us ever stronger to resist the onslaughts of the powers of darkness and triumph over these powers. The theology of the cross must be held in balance with the theology of glory. Though we live under the cross we have a foretaste of the glory that lies ahead of us. Through our own power we would fail ever again in the struggle against the Evil One, but through the conquering love of Christ we can persevere and overcome. Christian perfection is not so much the transcendence of sin as the victorious overcoming of sin.

Our conversion is both an event and a process. We enter the kingdom by being buried with Christ in the crisis of repentance and faith, but we must die daily as we put to death the evil desires that come into our hearts. Though we now live in the light, we must constantly endeavor to walk in the light and not succumb to the forces of darkness. We must take up the cross and mortify the flesh if we are to arrive at our final destination. Though we have faith, we must strive for holiness, for only in this way can we prove that our faith is real and living. We are justified only by faith, but we are not sanctified apart from works. Holiness of life is the invincible sign of the obedience of faith.

In contradistinction to much medieval mystical spirituality evangelicals stress a holiness in the world. Holiness does not consist in sublimely detaching oneself from the evils and discords of the world but in boldly confronting and unmasking these evils. It entails struggling with and overcoming the sinful distractions and temptations of life. Scriptural holiness is not the perfection of innocence in which one is shielded from the world but the victory of faith that overcomes the world (I Jn. 5:4). It does not impel one to turn away from the world but to seek to turn the world toward Christ. J. Gresham Machen expresses the evangelical ideal very well: "Instead of obliterating the distinction between the Kingdom and the world, or on the other hand withdrawing from the world into a sort of intellectual monasticism, let us go forth joyfully, enthusiastically, to make the world subject to God."[19] Surely Ignatius Loyola and the Society of Jesus share a similar vision, as do many other Catholic religious dedicated to the apostolate.

The Church's Spiritual Mission

Still another distinguishing mark of evangelicalism is its emphasis on the spiritual mission of the church. That the primary task of the church is to convert individuals, to bring the lost into the kingdom of God, has been affirmed by the great saints of both Catholicism and Protestantism. We need mention here only Bernard of Clairvaux, Aquinas, Loyola, Calvin, Luther, Wesley, Zinzendorf and William Carey. This conviction is based in part on the great commission given by the risen Christ to His disciples to go "into all the world and preach the gospel to the whole creation" (Mk. 16:15; cf. Mt. 28:19, 20; Lk. 10:2; Acts 1:8; 13:47). We as Christians are to have a burning concern to bring the message of salvation to all who are in bondage to the powers of darkness.

The commission given by Christ entails not only the preaching of the gospel but also teaching men to be disciples of our Lord (Mt. 28:19, 20). This is to say proclamation (*kerygma*) and teaching (*didache*) go together. The gospel and the law form a unity, though they are not to be equated. We are to preach the law as a guide for the Christian life and also as a spur to drive one to the gospel; the gospel in turn directs one ever again to the law.

To instruct men in the way of discipleship is also to

19 Quoted by N. B. Stonehouse in his *J. Gresham Machen* (Grand Rapids: Eerdmans, 1954), p. 187.

nurture them in the fellowship of the church. It is not enough to come to faith; one must grow in the faith toward spiritual maturity. This will entail the practice of the spiritual disciplines of which prayer is the most important. Prayer is indeed the soul of faith (Calvin).

Social service (*diakonia*) done in the name of Christ is also an integral part of the mission of the church. We are not only to follow Christ in a life of devotion and piety but also glorify Him in the service of our neighbor. Yet social service understood as corporal works of mercy is not to be put on the same level as prayer and the apostolate, which Thomas Aquinas termed "spiritual works of mercy." We read that the apostles perceived that it was not right to give up preaching the Word of God to serve at tables, and therefore the office of deacon was instituted to minister to the material needs of the Christian community (Acts 6). It is interesting to note that two of those enrolled as deacons, Philip and Stephen, became missionaries, presumably after fulfilling their *diakonia* duties.

It can be said that social service is a fruit and evidence of our faith and also a preparation for the proclamation of the faith. William Booth, founder of the Salvation Army, had as his motto "soup, soap and salvation." He saw that before men could be made ready to hear and receive the message of salvation something had to be done for their elemental physical and material needs. The pre-evangelism of works of mercy is often just as important as evangelism proper in bringing men into the kingdom of God.

Social action understood as political action is not an integral part of the church's mission, but it may very well be a supplement to this. Political action may be involved in the wider mission of the church, but this is primarily the responsibility of Christians in society rather than of the church per se. The church is called to convert individuals, not social structures. Yet Christians as citizens of the state will surely feel under an obligation to put the

Christian ethic in practice in daily life and seek social reforms.

The church as a church must speak to the critical moral issues in society through its preaching of the law. It must point directions, but as a general rule it should not issue political directives nor try to determine policy. This is the task of the state, which can also be a vehicle of the grace of God, though not of His saving grace.

Evangelical theology holds that the key to social amelioration is personal regeneration. It makes this affirmation against the Marxist view which says that if the social environment is changed then men will be changed. Yet discerning evangelicals acknowledge that personal regeneration by itself is not sufficient for the creation of a just society. In addition to personal conversion men must be taught about the social dimensions of sin and aroused to correct social abuses. The Christian must become sensitive to social as well as personal evils. He must be led to see that laws are necessary to hold sin in check and to assure equality of opportunity. We are not called out of the world but sent into the world as servants and ambassadors of Christ (Jn. 17:15, 18). Our spiritual vocation must be lived out in the secular society. The spiritual indeed is the foundation and goal of the secular. Our service in the secular realm has a spiritual aim, the bringing of lost men to Jesus Christ.

Dietrich Bonhoeffer, who is widely associated with the new secular theology, nevertheless saw that the church's mission is essentially spiritual. He declared that "the essence of the gospel does not lie in the solution to human problems, and . . . the solution of human problems cannot be the essential task of the Church. . . . the word of the Church is the call to conversion, the call to belief in the love of God in Christ, and the call to preparation for Christ's second coming and for the future kingdom of God."[20] He believed that in our preaching

[20] Dietrich Bonhoeffer, *Ethics.* Ed. Eberhard Bethge (N.Y.: Macmillan, 1965), pp. 356, 357.

we should relate to and challenge the critical social problems and issues of our time. He saw that authentic biblical preaching will have definite social and political implications, but its content is the word of salvation to lost sinners.

The Personal Return of Christ

Finally evangelical theology is noted for its affirmation of the visible coming again of Jesus Christ in power and glory to set up the kingdom that shall have no end. The hope of the Christian does not lie in a utopian society on earth but in the coming kingdom of God. It is not to be found in the secular city (as in Cox and Winter) but in the new Jerusalem coming down from heaven. Our hope is not a reformed world but a new heaven and a new earth. Against the tendency in much traditional Catholicism to equate the kingdom and the church, evangelicals hold that the kingdom is present in a proleptic fashion in the church but it is basically a future reality, one that will signalize the end of history and the judgment and purification of both church and world.

Though evangelicals are united in affirming the personal return of Christ, they have been divided concerning the exact relation between the coming kingdom and the present world. In reaction against the notion of a timeless eternity which is prevalent in both Roman Catholic and Protestant traditions, some evangelical Christians have entertained the idea of a millennial kingdom that gives substance to the prayer of Jesus that His will be done on earth as well as in heaven. The postmillennialists have seen this kingdom in terms of the spreading of Christian missions and the infusion of Christian values in the world before the second coming of Christ. The premillennialists envision an interim kingdom on earth inaugurated by the coming of Christ but preceding the final judgment and the kingdom of heaven. It seems to me that neither of these views does justice to the discontinuity between the old and new aeons, the kingdoms of this world and the coming kingdom of God. In this sense they have an affinity to the current theology of hope, which envisages a new social order as the future of our present world. Unlike the millennialists, however, the theologians of hope are reluctant to speak of the visible return of Jesus Christ or of any kind of supernatural intervention. Moreover, they understand the mission of the church in terms of social revolution rather than evangelism and in this respect approach the Marxist understanding of the coming kingdom of freedom.

To the credit of evangelical millenarianism it recovered a futuristic eschatology that had faded into the background in the period of the Reformation. Moreover, there is some truth in the concept of the millennium as it is portrayed in Revelation 20, though we believe that this must be interpreted symbolically, pertaining to a period within world history in which the rule of Christ will become more manifest. At the same time those who have championed millennial interpretations have often failed to affirm or take seriously the supernatural abodes of the dead, the interim states of Paradise and Hades and consequently also the doctrine of the communion of saints.

In summary we must say that the hope of the world lies in the end of the world. This will be realized in the personal, visible return of Jesus Christ as the conquering king. As it is stated in Hebrews 9:28: " . . . so Christ, having been offered once to bear the sins of many, will appear a second time, not to deal with sin but to save those who are eagerly waiting for him." We can and must work for social justice here on earth, for this is part of the Christian imperative, but social justice must not be confused with the righteousness of the kingdom, which can only be a gift of God. The mutual love that man can realize now in interpersonal relations is not to be equated with the sacrificial, outgoing love that will characterize the eternal kingdom.

The coming again of Christ will signify the judgment upon the world as well as the salvation of the body of the faithful. It will inaugurate the new heaven-earth and at the same time the terrible reality of hell, which nevertheless will not be outside the compass of divine grace. Those who stand under the wrath of God also stand under His love, even though this love is resisted. The day of the Lord will be a day of darkness as well as of light, and this is why the missionary imperative will remain until the end of historical time.

* * * * *

All the hallmarks that have been enumerated can also be found in other schools and branches of Christendom, but they have been given a special emphasis in the history of evangelicalism. Surely in Roman Catholicism they can all be detected, though we have acknowledged a definite evangelical strand within that communion. These distinguishing marks are significantly absent from liberal Protestant and neo-Catholic theologies, and most of them (though not all) are scarcely evident in Eastern Orthodoxy. They are certainly not dominant motifs in the theology and spirituality of the Eastern church, though this is not to deny that many of the treasures of the faith have been preserved in that communion.[21] With one or two exceptions these emphases are also conspicuously lacking in Anglo-Catholicism. Sect groups like the Jehovah's Witnesses and Mormons uphold a system of works-righteousness that stands at marked variance with the evangelical stress on free grace. The Virgin Birth and bodily resurrection of Christ have been prominent features of the creed of modern fundamentalism, but because they are stoutly affirmed by the Catholic branches of the faith and because they were not an essential part of the apologetic of the Protestant Reformation and of

---

[21] While the call to holiness figures prominently in Eastern Orthodoxy, the emphasis is much more on retirement from the world than on mission to the world.

evangelical Pietism, I did not feel that they should be included in this special list.

Opportunity for Evangelicals Today

As one surveys the contemporary cultural scene he cannot help but discern a spiritual dearth not only in the secular world but also in the churches and in church-related institutions, including colleges and seminaries. He will be constrained to acknowledge the growing influence of secular humanism even in the citadels of organized religion.

It is in light of this erosion of spiritual and especially Christian values that John Mackay, president emeritus of Princeton Seminary, has called for an evangelical renaissance which in his mind means the recovery of the centrality of the gospel of free grace, a personal relationship to Jesus Christ and the divine authority of the Scriptures in the churches of our land. It is only when the church itself is renewed and reformed that it can bring new life into a decaying secular culture. Only a church that has experienced a spiritual awakening can be a leaven in the world.

As has already been indicated in the first chapter, signs of an evangelical resurgence are numerous. For our purposes here we must caution against simply returning to old formulas of the past. There is a need to forge new creeds to combat the new heresies of our day. While maintaining continuity with the evangelical and Reformed tradition we must aim for a concrete, intelligible witness in our time.

Sectarianism has been one of the banes of evangelicalism in the past. This meant not only separation from the world but separation from other Christians. We should strive for a catholic evangelicalism, one that maintains continuity with the tradition of the whole church even while trying to correct and purify that tradition in the light of the Bible.

Evangelicals need also to be wary of an obscurantism that denies the valid insights of historical criticism and of a privatism that isolates faith from the social and political controversies of our time. Even more should we resist the insidious threat of acculturization, the accommodation to worldly values and standards. An evangelical renaissance will be aborted unless the dimension of the inner life is rediscovered. Doctrinal orthodoxy by itself cannot assure a revitalized church. What is needed is the recovery of the mystical and spiritual wellsprings of the faith, the renewal of the practice of the presence of God.

IV

A Reassessment of Karl Barth

A Word of Appreciation

Those who call themselves "evangelical" in the Anglo-Saxon countries generally regard the late Karl Barth with suspicion, since he does not echo and at some places diverges from the tradition of the Protestant Reformation. Barth, a pastor in the Reformed church of Switzerland before assuming a professorship at Basel University, is known for his defense of Reformed Protestantism against both Roman Catholicism and modernism, and yet he has not been fully accepted in the evangelical world. It should be noted that no creative and original theologian has ever been popular with his peers and only slightly less with the church at large. Some on the conservative evangelical spectrum have assailed Barth, accusing him of a "new modernism" (Van Til, J. W. Montgomery, Harold Brown). Others have valued his contribution and sought to appropriate his genuinely biblical insights (Colin Brown, Berkouwer, Runia, K. Hamilton).

While openly questioning much of what Barth says, we think that it is possible to appreciate some of his novel and daring formulations of the age-old truths of the Bible. Even though not wishing to be known as Barthian or neo-Barthian, we believe that Barth must be taken with the utmost seriousness by any theologian of evangelical or Reformed persuasion. Barth is not only the foremost Protestant thinker of this century but also probably the most profound and influential Christian theologian of our age.

First of all it should be said that Karl Barth is himself an evangelical theologian. His little book *Evangelical Theology* with its forthright call for Scriptural authority and personal commitment should be read by all who desire to learn from this great scholar. His monumental *Church Dogmatics* is anchored in a deep study of the Scriptures and is replete with Scriptural references.

Evangelicals can stand with Barth in his call for a theology of revelation, which he sharply differentiates from philosophical theology and philosophy of religion. A theology of revelation is based upon the Word of God in Scripture and not upon human wisdom and imagination. Though Barth acknowledges the universal presence of God, he denies any place to natural theology, since true knowledge of God is gained only when God makes Himself known by His Word and Spirit.

Barth is firm in his commitment to the authority of the Bible, but he does not identify the letter of Scripture with the revealed Word of God. He maintains that the Bible is the sole and original source and medium of revelation, and in this sense he upholds *sola Scriptura*. The tradition of the church must be measured by Scripture and not vice versa.

Barth's criterion is the Word and Spirit. The Bible as the written Word becomes revelation when the Spirit discloses its infallible truth to the minds of believers. God has spoken His Word once for all to the prophets and apostles, and He is free to speak His Word anew in every generation. Though Barth accepts the principle of historical or higher criticism, he is adamant that criticism never procures for man the Word of God or the truth of revelation. The most that criticism can do is to throw light upon the historical and cultural background of the biblical text or passage. God's Word is never available to human reason. In order for one to hear His Word God must speak through the Scriptures and act upon the human heart. Barth declares: "God's Word is never 'available' for anyone. God's Word is God's Spirit, who blows where He will."[1]

His Calvinist heritage is again evident in his strong insistence upon the sovereignty of God. God can never be mastered or controlled by the human will; even in partnership with man God remains Lord and Master. Barth does not defend the impassible God of Greek speculation, for God enters into human history and shares our weakness and tribulation in the person of His Son Jesus Christ. At the same time he will have nothing to do with the modernist idea of a finite or growing God who is essentially dependent on man and the world.

Barth is also to be commended for affirming the wrath and holiness of God as well as His love. Unlike some latter-day Calvinists, however, he refuses to separate God's love from His wrath. For this theologian God's wrath is one form of His love; His judgment is only another manifestation of His grace. In our view Barth is here more biblical and genuinely Christian than some of his opponents.

Barth also affirms the triumph of the grace of God, which will finally put an end to sin, death and suffering. As we shall try to show, he does not fully perceive that God's grace can be triumphant even in rejection and damnation, though he does not totally foreclose this possibility. Barth's doctrine of the triumph of grace is founded on his belief in the universal atonement of Christ. In the Barthian perspective Christ dies for all men and not just for a select number of the specially favored.

Again it should be recognized that Barth stands firmly within the catholic faith in his ardent espousal of the substitutionary atonement of Christ. It was because Jesus

---

[1] Karl Barth, *God Here and Now*. Trans. Paul Van Buren (London: Routledge & Kegan Paul, 1964), p. 54.

Christ, God's own Son, died in our place that our sins are forgiven and that we are set free from the powers of darkness. This means that we are justified solely by the grace of God and not by the meritorious works of man.

Barth's defense of the Virgin Birth of Christ and His bodily resurrection likewise marks him as an evangelical. To be sure he insists that these miracles cannot be corroborated by historical science, that they are matters of "sacred history" rather than of mere objective history. Yet we must remember that only faith and not empirical observation can discern the hand of God in a miraculous event, and this is what Barth is trying to underscore.

His brilliant exposition of the doctrine of the trinity should also be appreciated by those of an orthodox persuasion, though he rightly contends that this doctrine is not a revealed truth but an immediate implication of the fact, form and content of revelation. It is not a synthesis or reconciliation of several diverse elements in the Bible but instead an analytical development of the central fact of revelation. In contradistinction to many neo-liberals Barth affirms the ontological or immanent trinity and not simply the economic trinity in which God is depicted as triune only in His activity or in His relationship to man. Barth prefers to speak of "modes of Being" rather than of "persons" in the trinitarian relationship. Yet it is unjust to accuse him of modalism, since he affirms distinctions within God Himself.

Finally Barth's understanding of prayer as being primarily and essentially heartfelt supplication before a holy and merciful God can surely be recognized as biblical and evangelical. In the circles of mysticism prayer is depicted as contemplative adoration and meditation on a spiritual theme. In radical-secular theology prayer is seen as reflection upon the needs of the world and then rising to meet these needs. But because Barth adheres to a personal God, to the living God of Scripture, he sees prayer as conversation and petition; the petitionary element is present, he contends, even in adoration and thanksgiving.

Some Reservations

Although Barth can be considered for the most part to be an evangelical theologian, this is not to gainsay that there are nonbiblical and even philosophical elements in his theology. He has a biblical side and a rationalistic side. He basically stands in the tradition of the Reformation, but other influences impinge on his thought, including Platonism and the Enlightenment, and these at times obscure his essentially biblical orientation.

The first place where we have difficulty with Barth is in his contention that there is no natural knowledge of God, that God can be known only as He gives Himself to be known in the event of revelation. In contrast to Barth we affirm that man does have a natural knowledge of God, though this is a broken and inadequate knowledge and leads not to salvation but to condemnation. Such knowledge is not a stepping stone to faith but instead the antithesis to faith. It renders man inexcusable, and this is why man merits condemnation rather than salvation. He knows the truth but he does not do it (Rom. 1, 2). By denying a bona fide natural knowledge of God Barth cannot hold the natural man responsible for his misdeeds. Ellul, who follows Barth here, describes the ethics of the natural man as an ethics of necessity. We affirm that man is responsible not only in faith but also apart from faith. In the later volumes of his dogmatics Barth affirms that every man is a hearer of the Word of God, but this is not a natural knowledge but a knowledge given to him by the universal Christ. He also refers to "lights and truths" in creation which man can discern on his own apart from faith, but they do not yield a true or valid knowledge of God and are not sufficient for the construction of a natural theology.

Barth declares: "To be apprehended is enough. It requires no correlative on my side, and can have none."[2] In my estimation this is manifestly unbiblical, since it denies the necessity of personal faith and commitment for salvation. Barth holds that faith is an acknowledgment of what God has done for us in Christ, but that faith itself is not an event of salvation. We hold on the basis of Scripture that our salvation is both objective and subjective; its ground and center are in the cross of Calvary, but its realization and fulfillment lie in bearing the cross in a life of faith. "For God so loved the world that he gave his only Son, that whoever believes in him should not perish but have eternal life" (Jn. 3:16). The indissoluble connection between the obedience of faith and salvation is further underscored in verse 36 of the third chapter of John: "He who believes in the Son has eternal life; he who does not obey the Son shall not see life, but the wrath of God rests upon him."

It can be seen that Barth's historical objectivism is the basis for his doctrine of universal salvation. Men are not only saved by Christ *de jure* (in principle) but *de facto* (in fact).[3] To be sure they must respond to the salvation of Christ in a life of faith and service, but this response has ethical more than soteriological significance. Barth admits that though all men are predestined in Christ, they can resist their predestination or election, but he firmly doubts that they can do so forever. He stops short of affirming a universal restoration of all to God, but the implications of his theology drive him in this direction. He writes that "all men and all creation . . . are ordained

[2] Karl Barth, *The Epistle to the Philippians* (Richmond: John Knox, 1962), p. 108.

[3] "As the one thing which has to be done it is already wholly and utterly accomplished in Him. As that which has taken place in God—in which we are indeed participators on the strength of the nature of the person and work of Jesus Christ—it is in itself and from the very outset something which has taken place to and in us." Karl Barth, *Church Dogmatics*, II, 2 (Edinburgh: T. & T. Clark, 1957), p. 158.

to be the theaters of His glory and therefore to be recipients and bearers of His Word."[4] Men nevertheless can defy and deny their election and salvation, but God is faithful even when men are faithless, and God's grace cannot forever be thwarted. Barth does not wish to compromise the sovereign freedom of God by tying His grace to the principle of universal restoration (*apokatastasis*), but he is adamant in his conviction that no man can escape from God's all-encompassing love nor undo the decision of His gracious election.

If Barth would give adequate recognition to the truth that God's grace can still be triumphant even in the denial of His grace, that hell too can be consonant with His grace and love, then he would not necessarily be in the camp of universalism. There are some passages in which Barth does recognize the possibility of hell coexisting with the love of God, but for him this is a state in the present rather than a revelation of the destiny of wilful unbelievers.

Barth's objectivistic universalism has decided implications in the area of preaching. Our mission as spokesmen for Christ, he maintains, is not to save souls but to exalt Christ. Preaching can bring people to an awareness of the gift of salvation already won for them, but it cannot actually convey salvation to people. In his view: "Even with the most powerful and heartfelt appeal which it [preaching] may make to them, it cannot change men. But with its appeal it can set before them the act of the love of God in which He has already changed them."[5] This general position certainly conflicts with that of St. Paul: "I have become all things to all men, that I might by all means save some" (I Cor. 9:22; cf. I Tim. 4:16). It also stands in tension with that of Jude: "And convince

---

[4] Karl Barth, *Church Dogmatics*, IV, 3, a (Edinburgh: T. & T. Clark, 1961), p. 117.

[5] Karl Barth, *Church Dogmatics*, IV, 3, b (Edinburgh: T. & T. Clark, 1962), p. 852.

some who doubt; save some, by snatching them out of the fire" (Jude 22, 23; cf. Jms. 5:20).

Before dismissing Barth's universalism it should be noted that there can be a true universalism on the basis of Scripture just as there can be a false particularism. We cannot subscribe to the view of some of the older Calvinists that Christ died only for the elect and not for the whole world. We must hold that the death of Christ benefits all men, though in different ways. Even unbelievers are claimed by the love of Christ, even they are included in the saving plan of Christ (cf. I Tim. 4:10), but their persistent refusal to repent of sin and believe in Christ marks them for condemnation.

It should be recognized that the doctrine of the universal atonement can be detected in many spiritual writers of the past, including some staunch evangelicals. Oswald Chambers, the evangelical Baptist preacher and missionary in early twentieth-century England, wrote: "I am not saved by believing; I realize I am saved by believing. It is not repentance that saves me; repentance is the sign that I realize what God has done in Christ Jesus."[6] Chambers held to a universal atonement but also to the possibility of damnation, for one can reject the salvation of Christ. "In the cross of Jesus Christ God redeemed the whole human race from the possibility of damnation through the heredity of sin; but if, when I realize that Jesus Christ came to deliver me from the wrong disposition by putting in a right one, I refuse to let Him do it, that moment my condemnation begins."[7]

In our position salvation is realized both in the cross of Christ and the decision of faith, but only those who have faith can legitimately claim that they were already redeemed at the cross of Calvary. Salvation and faith are correlative, as Berkouwer cogently reminds us in his stim-

[6] Oswald Chambers, *My Utmost for His Highest*, p. 302.
[7] Oswald Chambers, *In the Shadow of an Agony* (London: Complete Press, 1920), p. 98.

ulating work *Faith and Justification*, and trouble ensues
when these are separated. The goal of salvation is eternal
glory inaugurated by the last judgment, which is not
simply the revelation of what already is, as Barth would
have it, but instead the fulfillment and consummation of
God's saving purpose.

Many of those who adhere to a biblical orientation will
also find fault with Barth's theory of evil. In Barthian
theology the source of evil lies in the chaos, the nothingness which God does not will but which thereby is given a
temporal or provisional reality. When God created the
world, He separated the light from the darkness or the
chaos that was not pre-existent material but instead an
excluded possibility that God allowed a kind of shadowy
existence. The darkness or the chaos does not represent
being but nonbeing. It signifies the absence of light,
privation and deficiency, though it assumes a more sinis-
ter character when it tempts man to turn away from the
light and follow his own conceit. Barth's doctrine of evil,
it seems to me, is more Platonic than biblical, since he
traces the ultimate source of evil to nonbeing rather than
to demonic sin. The devils in his system are not fallen
angels but are only symbolic of the chaos in its dynamic
manifestation.

Is the chaos or nothingness a real adversary of God or
does it pose a threat only to God's creation, to man and
his civilization? Barth declares:

> It [the chaos] is not an adversary to God, but only the
> shadow of His work which both arises and is at once dis-
> pelled by His wrath. But to the creature it is an adversary for
> which the creature as such is no match. To God it is no
> problem. But it is a radical problem which faces the crea-
> ture.[8]

In the later sections of his *Church Dogmatics*, III, 2
Barth says that God treats the nothingness as an adversary because it challenges and threatens His creation. It

[8] Karl Barth, *Church Dogmatics*, III, 2 (Edinburgh: T. & T. Clark, 1960),
p. 77.

stands in opposition to God, but this opposition is effective only in the world of the creature. God Himself stands above the antithesis between the chaos and the creation, but He enters into this antithesis and makes the cause of the creature His own, overcoming and destroying the nothingness within the sphere of humanity. Yet for Barth even before the cross of Christ God's No reduces evil to impotence while at the same time giving it a kind of negative reality.[9] He also says that in the light of the cross of Christ the principalities and powers are no longer the enemies of God but now His servants. Though the nothingness was given for a time the role of an adversary to God, after Christ it has been shorn of its power and efficacy. He declares: "In the light of Jesus Christ there is no sense in which it can be affirmed that nothingness has any objective existence, that it continues except for our still blinded eyes, that it is still to be feared, that it still counts as a cogent factor . . . that it still implies a threat and possesses destructive power."[10] Yet it continues to have a semblance of power because of man's slowness in recognizing the victory of Christ. Barth seems to imply that the locus of evil after the victory of Christ is in man's ignorance and that what man needs is enlightenment.

This brings us to Barth's unwarranted optimism, an optimism based not only on the "unreality" or powerlessness of the adversary of God and man but also on the nature of man. For Barth man is basically good, even though he time and again falls into sin. But even in sin man "has not lost—even in part—the good nature which was created by God."[11] Sin obscures but does not alter man's real nature.

---

9 "God does not have to contend with it [the chaos] for the mastery. . . . For as soon as it entered the world it came under His dominion." *Ibid.*, p. 616.

10 Karl Barth, *Church Dogmatics*, III, 3 (Edinburgh: T. & T. Clark, 1960), p. 363.

11 Karl Barth, *Church Dogmatics*, IV, 1 (Edinburgh: T. & T. Clark, 1969), p. 492.

Barth is more prone to speak of the "real man" who is hidden by sin than of the "old man" who is corrupted by sin. Barth does refer to the latter, but he insists that the "old man" is in the past; he has been done away with at the cross of Calvary.[12]   The only possibility now open to man is Jesus Christ, "the new man" in whom we are already included by virtue of the universal atonement of Christ. Sin is an "ontological impossibility" that occurs despite man's basic orientation toward good. Barth acknowledges that in sinning men lose their freedom, but because God's grace is ever available, man can recover his original freedom and realize his true nature in obedience to Christ. Barth's position contravenes that of Reformation orthodoxy, which sees man as originally good but after the fall under the sway of the powers of sin and darkness. His essential nature is good, but his present or existential nature is corrupt and incapable of any good thing in the sight of God.

One implication of Barth's universalism and this-worldly optimism is that he does not take unbelief with the utmost seriousness. Unbelievers are only sadly misguided persons who do not see their true status as children of God. Their sins are not especially heinous in the sight of God, since "before God everything is impure; and therefore nothing is especially impure."[13]   Their reasoning is not so much perverse as inadequate, not so much deceptive as misdirected. The secular philosopher should be regarded as the advocate of man and the world (advocatus hominis et mundi), not an instrument of the devil (advocatus diaboli). Von Balthasar interprets Barth as holding that since "every man is a hearer of the Word . . . the unbelief of the sinner can be nothing but a vain, already quashed rebellion against the truth of God within him."[14]   In Barth's view unbelief sometimes needs to

[12] Barth states that "there is no more place for the old man," for he has been "replaced by the new." Church Dogmatics, IV, 1, p. 557.

[13] Karl Barth, The Epistle to the Romans, p. 517.

[14] Hans Urs von Balthasar, The Theology of Karl Barth, p. 202.

be ignored, whereas we hold that it needs to be overthrown by the law and the gospel.

For Barth it would seem that our legs are bruised by the fall, not broken, but we act as if they were broken. Man is ontologically and morally capable of deciding for Christ, but he does not have the will to do so. He has an openness for God's revelation by virtue of his creation in God's image, but not a readiness or willingness for it. His fears and doubts need to be dispelled, and this is why he needs to hear the good news that he has been accepted and forgiven by God in Jesus Christ.

Barth has lent his prestige to the Christian-Marxist dialogue because he believes that Christians and Communists are already virtual brothers. They can work toward common goals because they are bound together in Christ, even though this bond of unity is not acknowledged by one of the parties. Reinhold Niebuhr has probably been more perceptive in his diagnosis of Communism, describing it as "the noxious demonry" of a "worldwide secular religion."[15] At the same time it should be noted that much of Barth's advice on the Christian approach to Marxism has been intended for Christians living in Marxist lands, and coexistence may be a more realistic alternative for such persons than outright opposition.

Barth sees the world as already redeemed and the powers of darkness as already destroyed. He sees man as being already a child of God, and he sees the grace of God filling the whole earth. Thielicke is probably right when he accuses Barth of sundering the biblical dualism between light and darkness, faith and unbelief, heaven and hell. Barth is closer to the monism of the Enlightenment which sees reality as basically good, since for him it is all encompassed in Christ.

Are Thielicke and some other critics of Barth on solid ground when they accuse him of "Christomonism"? It

15 Reinhold Niebuhr, *Christian Realism and Political Problems* (N.Y.: Charles Scribner's Sons, 1953), p. 34.

should be noted that Barth repudiates this label, and much of what he says would seem to support his disclaimer. He avers: "Not the cosmos is the Son or Word of God, but the unique One whom He sends into the world as His Son and therefore His Word. Not every man is a Christ, but Jesus of Nazareth alone."[16] Yet he contends that all men and the whole world are in Christ, though Christ is not yet in all men. "He, the living Jesus Christ, is the circle enclosing all men and every man . . . the circle of divine judgment and divine grace." Already in his *Epistle to the Romans*, which brought him into the limelight, he speaks of the omnipresence of Jesus Christ in the world, and for this he has been accused by von Balthasar of "theopanism." He declares that in the light of the obedience of Jesus Christ "there is no man who is not—in Christ. All are renewed and clothed with righteousness, all are become a new subject, and are therefore set at liberty and placed under the affirmation of God."[17] Yet such passages are counterbalanced by his awareness that all men are not yet in the covenant community of God, that all men have not yet been baptized by the Holy Spirit into the body of Christ, and this too must be taken into consideration in our final assessment of this theologian.

Besides the dispute over Christomonism many conservatives are disturbed about Barth's doctrine of Scripture. He affirms both the divine infallibility and human fallibility of the Bible, but it is not clear exactly what he means by these terms. On the one hand he declares that the Bible gives "infallible information" concerning God and His will and purpose for the world, and on the other he states that the Bible is susceptible to error not only in its historical and scientific but also in its theological statements. He seems to mean that when the Bible is taken as a whole, it gives a reliable and trustworthy

16 *Church Dogmatics*, IV, 3, a, p. 222.
17 Karl Barth, *The Epistle to the Romans*, p. 182.

picture of God and His gospel, but when a text is treated only in its limited context, then its interpretation is inadequate or deficient and needs to be supplemented. He also appears to have in mind that the biblical writers, being wholly human, were conditioned by their cultural and historical backgrounds and therefore were incapable of seeing the whole truth from their partial vantage points. One might say that for Barth the Bible is functionally adequate in that it is capable of bringing to men the truth of the gospel but that it is not necessarily dependable in everything that it reports. It is basically truthful and authoritative despite its external flaws. Barth opposes the theory of verbal inspiration as traditionally stated because in his view it freezes the Word of God in human propositions; he prefers to reinterpret inspiration in dynamic terms, making a place for the Spirit's guidance of the writers but also including the reception of the Word of God by the readers.

What are we to say to all this? First it cannot be doubted that the writers wrote out of a limited perspective and that their particular truths need to be seen in the context of the whole of Scripture. At the same time this should not be taken to mean that they were in error in their basic witness, in what they were led to describe or proclaim. Being human they certainly had a capacity for error, but must not we affirm that the Spirit truly guided them in their discernment and rendition of the will and purpose of God? Otherwise inspiration begins to lose its meaning and impact. Their interpretation may need to be qualified and supplemented, but we cannot say that in its basic thrust it needs to be reformed or corrected if what they wrote was indeed the Word of God. In practice Barth seems to take for granted the essential reliability and trustworthiness of Scripture, but in principle he allows for errors even in the matters of theological judgment.

We concur with Barth that the truth of the Bible is not self-evident, and this is where rationalistic fundamentalists go astray. The revelatory norm is not simply available to human perception. To see the text in the light of the overall interpretation of Scripture is a divine but not a human possibility. To apprehend the truth of revelation one's spiritual eyes must be opened from within by the Holy Spirit.

This brings us to Barth's understanding of the means of grace. Though originally he made use of this concept, he came to regard it as not representative of the truth that he was trying to declare. Neither the Bible nor the sermon can be regarded as a means of grace, since God is free to speak His Word without these means. Moreover, when God does use human instrumentality He always acts in conjunction with the human word but never in and through it.[18] This means that the Bible and the sermon, as well as the sacraments, are signs and witnesses to grace, more than means of grace. They testify to a grace already poured out for man in Jesus Christ. They are aids by which we become aware of the grace of Christ, but they in themselves do not convey or communicate saving grace. The sacraments are not recognized as such by Barth; they are ordinances of the church testifying to the event of God's reconciliation in the past and man's dedication in the present.

Finally we come to Barth's alleged ahistorical orientation. It is commonly said by many of his critics that he deemphasizes history. This is much more true of his earlier than of his later works, where he becomes more futuristic and ostensibly historical. In his earlier phase he persists in maintaining that there is nothing in history as such on which faith can ground itself. The Word of God is eternity breaking into time and never itself becoming timebound or historical. The moment of revelation, he says, has no continuity with the before and after; it is always wholly new. History is revelation as "primal his-

[18] "God's action never takes place 'in and under.' It certainly takes place 'with' man's activity, but also above and in face of it." Karl Barth, *Church Dogmatics*, III, 4 (Edinburgh: T. & T. Clark, 1961), p. 521.

tory," history viewed in the light of its "nonhistorical radiance."

In his *Church Dogmatics*, particularly in the later volumes, Barth's orientation is much more historical; he even maintains that God has a history of His own, which is nevertheless qualitatively distinct from earthly history. He is adamant that God indeed entered into human history in the person of Jesus of Nazareth while still remaining the eternal God. At the same time he prefers to speak of the Word "assuming" human flesh instead of "becoming flesh." Likewise the Word of God did not itself become the words in the Bible nor do the body and blood of Christ in the sacrament really enter into the bread and wine.

Barth is correct that the heavenly Word is not to be equated with the human flesh of Jesus nor does it have a one-to-one identity with the words in the Bible or the elements in the sacrament. But cannot we say that there is a direct and inseparable connection between the Word of God and Jesus, and should not we go on to affirm that the Word of God is truly "in, with and under" the words of the Bible as well as the bread and wine in the sacrament? If there is a real incarnation this means that the Word of God must have become in some sense historical, for otherwise we are forced to the conclusion that the Word only appeared in Jesus or was reflected in Him to a high degree. Barth is more ready to acknowledge the real presence of God in the historical Jesus than in the proclamation and sacraments of the church. He stoutly affirms the hypostatic union between the Word of God and Jesus, but refuses to posit an integral relationship between the presence of the Word and what are traditionally known as "the means of grace."

Certainly the early Barth seems very much bound to the older Reformed formula *finitum non capax infiniti* (the finite cannot receive and bear the infinite). In his stress on the utter transcendence of God, it seems that man never really gains a valid perception of God nor ever really participates in His presence and activity. In his later writings, especially in his *The Humanity of God*, Barth appears to have broken with this formula, though he continues to emphasize that God is present with us only in Jesus Christ and His Spirit, not in the sacraments of the church nor in verbal propositions. If we would be rigidly bound to the formula *finitum non capax infiniti*, we would be compelled to conclude that the Word is not really expressed in but only unveiled through the Bible or the sermon. Nor can it ever be embodied in the sacramental rite but only proclaimed by this rite. This seems to be Barth's position not only in regard to the sermon and the sacraments but also to the Christian life. For Barth the Christian should never be thought of as "a little Christ" (as in Luther) but rather as a servant and herald of Christ.

The truth in the controversial formula *finitum non capax infiniti* is that in ourselves we are lamentably unable to receive and convey the Word of God, but by His Spirit we are inwardly empowered to appropriate and to communicate the saving truth of God's revelation. We can never wholly assimilate this truth because it stands at variance with human reason; the central mysteries of the faith defy human logic. Yet even though God's Word eludes our comprehension we can truly know it—know it well enough to relate it to our life and world and to tell others about it. Barth would here very probably be in agreement.

Concluding Appraisal

Barth's attempt to recover the primal authority of Scripture and at the same time avoid the bibliolatry that is a perennial conservative temptation is to be applauded. We need to see the humanity as well as the divinity of the Bible and recognize that it is through very human words that we hear the voice of the living God. What is infallible is not the text as such but the message or the truth that the text conveys and proclaims. Barth reminds us of the cultural and historical limitations of the biblical authors, and this is a much needed corrective to the Monophysite doctrine of Scripture in vogue in certain circles of orthodoxy in which the human nature of Scripture is swallowed up in its divine nature.[19]

At the same time we must insist that the Bible truly presents to us God's Word; it does not merely point to a transcendent Word that is incapable of human definition and formulation. The divine Word is not only witnessed to by the human word but embodied in it. The divine truth comes to us in propositional form as well as in the form of personal encounter. We must also hold with Calvin that the biblical Word is not only an instrument but also the object of the Spirit's witness.

His emphasis on the universal Lordship of Christ is also to be appreciated in a time when sovereignty is being invested in the will of the nation or of the people. At the same time Barth's conception of Christocracy in which Christ's kingdom is pictured as now embracing the whole world does not coincide with the biblical view that the world is enemy-occupied territory, that the devil is still in some sense the prince of the world. Christ rules through and over the devil to be sure, but this is His alien work, not His proper work which is exercised through the ministry of the Word. He is Lord of the whole world only in a hidden and indirect way by virtue of His union with the Father and His resurrection triumph, but He has not yet established His Lordship in the hearts of all men. Christ is truly sovereign, but only where His kingship is acknowledged can His kingdom be said to exist.

Barth tends to deny that the warfare between God and the devil still continues, since the devil has been overthrown by Jesus Christ.[20] The chaos after Christ, he says,

---

[19] It should be noted that many conservatives also affirm the omniscience of the earthly Jesus, thereby losing sight of His essential humanity.

[20] In some places Barth qualifies his general position that the victory of Christ over the powers of darkness was total and final. He writes: "The power of light is not so overwhelming in relation to that of darkness that

has "only the force of a dangerous appearance."[21] He
contends that it is the opinion of a "fanatical Pietism"
that the world "stands under the dominion of the devil,"
though this is precisely what is affirmed in I John 5:19.
For him "this kingdom [of darkness] is behind us and all
men. We and all men are released from this prison."[22]

The Barthian error is that the world is said to be
already redeemed. We see the world on the contrary as a
perennial battleground between the forces of light and
darkness. The devil has been mortally wounded by the
cross and resurrection victory of Christ, but by virtue of
this fact he has become even more dangerous. Barth
could not say as did Jonathan Edwards: "Satan will keep
men secure as long as he can; but when he can do that no
longer, he often endeavours to drive them to extremes,
and so to dishonour God and wound religion in that
way."[23] For Barth the power of the devil is a mirage; he
is likened to "a wasp without a sting." In our view Satan
does not have the power to overthrow faith, but he does
have the power to work disease, sin and death in the
world and even to cast believers into prison (cf. Rev.
2:10).

Barth reminds us that the ground of our assurance is
Christ Himself and His promises in Holy Scripture. Our
assurance is not to be based on our own experience nor
on rational signs and evidences. While basically concur-
ring with Barth we hold that the mystical or experiential
dimension of faith is not to be neglected. Experience is
not the source of our faith, but it is an integral element in
faith. Can we be said to be Christians unless we have

---

darkness has lost its power altogether. . . . Light still battles with darkness,
with the resisting element in man, with the prince of darkness." *Church
Dogmatics*, IV, 3, a, pp. 168, 262. Yet Barth sees this conflict more in terms
of a mopping-up operation than of a continuing warfare.

[21] Barth, *Church Dogmatics*, IV, 1, p. 506.

[22] *Ibid.*, p. 503.

[23] Jonathan Edwards, *Marks of a Work of the Spirit* in *The Works of
President Edwards*, Vol. III (N.Y.: G. & C. & H. Carvill, 1830), p. 595.

experienced the wrath of God against sin as well as His love and mercy shown forth in Jesus Christ?

Barth's predilection for objectivity is especially evident in his soteriology where salvation is depicted as something that has happened to us in the past. For him the Christian is summoned to vocation, not salvation. He insists that not only the possibility but the very reality of salvation was procured for us at Calvary. As we have already said, this point of view is valid if it is made to refer only to believers. We must go on to contend that though salvation has a past dimension it also has a present dimension. It is an accomplished fact but at the same time something to be fought for and recovered in the here and now. The Christian life has not only ethical but also soteriological significance, since apart from a living and active faith our salvation will gradually vanish away, as Calvin said.[24] We are not here upholding a theology of works-righteousness, since our good works as well as our faith are the result of the Holy Spirit working in and through us. Barth speaks much of the role of the Holy Spirit, but for him the Spirit reveals what has already happened to man in Jesus Christ. We contend that the Spirit applies the salvation of Christ to the hearts of believers.

Barth wishes to stand with the Reformation in its affirmation of salvation by grace (*sola gratia*) and justification by faith alone (*sola fide*), but can he hold to the latter consistently and thoroughly in the light of his doctrine of universal justification? We regard him as a brother within the evangelical and Reformed family but one who perhaps at times has sought to be too inclusive, too open to the world. At the same time we need to be reminded that God's love extends to all and that His salvation is offered for all, though in the mystery of His providence not all accept this offer.

In my estimation one has the right to criticize Barth

[24] John Calvin, *Institutes*, II, 16, 1.

only when one sees the errors that he warns against and seeks to counteract. Barth's contribution to the contemporary theological discussion must be taken seriously. This great theologian cannot be dismissed, for too much of what he says rings true. Even those who find themselves in serious disagreement with him would benefit from wrestling with his works. His strong Christocentric emphasis by which he upholds Jesus Christ as true God and true man is much needed in a time of creeping unitarianism and growing syncretism. His staunch affirmation of the sovereignty and freedom of God is a welcome corrective to the varied attempts of modern folk religion to domesticate and control God. Our conclusion is that though he does not wholly succeed in holding in balance various emphases in the Bible he is to be reckoned as one of the theological giants of our age and all ages.

V

The Legacy of Pietism

In the recent past a decided antipathy toward Pietism can be detected in both conservative and liberal circles. Secular theologians like Gibson Winter and Harvey Cox accuse Pietism of otherworldliness. Gordon Clark, conservative Calvinist, decries the irrationalist tendency in Pietism. In his 1919 *Commentary on Romans* Karl Barth speaks of "the inferno of pietism in which the demons do their work."

A common criticism one hears is that the Pietists stressed personal salvation to the detriment of social service. Joseph Fletcher voices the complaint that Pietism tended to separate faith from the crucial issues of society and daily life.[1] Martin Marty makes a similar charge: "For all its glories, Pietism was one of the major strides of Christian retreat from responsibility as it had been viewed in the past."[1a] Yet this is a serious misconception, for it can be shown that the leaders of the Pietist movement definitely promoted social concern, even becoming involved at times in political action.

It is also commonly said that the Pietists disparaged the intellect. Yet they not only promoted Bible study

[1] Joseph Fletcher, *Situation Ethics* (Philadelphia: Westminster, 1966), pp. 160, 161.

[1a] Martin Marty, *A Short History of Christianity* (Cleveland: World, 1959), p. 275.

among laymen but also established a great many educational institutions, colleges as well as seminaries. Men like Spener, John Owen, Jonathan Edwards and Bengel were both profound thinkers and prolific writers. Kierkegaard, who is probably closer to Pietism than to confessional Lutheranism, is also worthy of mention in this connection.[2]

Pietism has often been confused with fundamentalism, which signifies a synthesis of latter-day Pietism and scholastic orthodoxy. The fundamentalists kept alive some of the concerns in the original movement of Pietism, but other concerns were obscured. The defensive posture of fundamentalism made it very difficult for both its supporters and its critics to recognize and appreciate the catholic and ecumenical dimensions within Pietism.

Many scholars are now having second thoughts on Pietism. Karl Barth, who is noted for his stricture against Pietism in his earlier writings, has said that the present need is for a rediscovery of Zinzendorf with his Christ-centered emphasis. Jaroslav Pelikan sees in Pietism a rebirth of the ethical concerns that were dissipated by the Thirty Years War and the rise of formalistic religion. Emil Brunner in his *The Divine-Human Encounter* mentions the indebtedness of the dialectic theologians to two great figures of Pietism—Christoph Blumhardt and Kierkegaard.

That the bogey of Pietism is being dissipated is evident in the appearance of new books on Pietism and Puritanism and the reissuing of some of the classics of Pietism, such as Philip Spener's *Pia Desideria* and Zinzendorf's *Nine Public Lectures on Important Subjects in Religion*.[3] We might also mention in this connection the

_____

[2] The influence of Pietism can also be discerned in Schleiermacher and Kant, though they are essentially children of the Enlightenment, despite their attempts to transcend it. Schleiermacher is more mystical and idealistic than evangelical, and Kant is more rationalistic.

[3] See Philip Spener, *Pia Desideria*. Trans. Theodore G. Tappert (Philadelphia: Fortress, 1964); and George Forell, ed. and trans., *Zinzendorf: Nine Public Lectures on Important Subjects in Religion* (Iowa City: Univ. of Iowa Press, 1973).

republishing of Foxe's *Book of Martyrs* and Ernest Gordon's *A Book of Protestant Saints,* which concerns Pietism in the nineteenth and early twentieth centuries. Interestingly enough Albrecht Ritschl's monumental *Geschichte des Pietismus* (*History of Pietism*) was reissued in 1966, though there is general agreement that his treatment of the movement was not altogether fair. Also noteworthy are such relatively new books on the subject of Pietism as A. J. Lewis's *Zinzendorf: The Ecumenical Pioneer* (Westminster, 1962) and F. Ernest Stoeffler's *The Rise of Evangelical Pietism* (Brill, 1965). The revival of interest in the kindred movements of Puritanism and Evangelicalism is also apparent in the reissuing of many of the Puritan classics.

How should Pietism be defined? In the narrow sense it signifies the movement for spiritual renewal that sprang out of the Lutheran and Reformed churches in continental Europe in the seventeenth and eighteenth centuries. Among its luminaries were Philip Spener, Johann Arndt, August Francke, Willem Tellinck, Gilbertus Voetius, Jodocus von Lodensteyn, Theodore Brakel, William à Brakel, Frederick Lampe, Zinzendorf, Philip Otterbein, Johann Bengel, Tersteegen, Johann Neander and Theodor Untereyck. The later flowering of the Pietistic movement includes Robert Haldane, Frederic Godet, Anna Schlatter, Johann Lavater, Christian Spittler, Theodore Fliedner, Cesar Malan, Adolphe Monod, Alexander Morel, Carl and Dora Rappard, Gottfried Krummacher, Friedrich von Bodelschwingh, Carl Olaf Rosenius, Hans Nielsen Hauge, O. Hallesby, the Blumhardts and probably Kierkegaard. Abraham Kuyper too was markedly affected by the Pietist awakening, though he became highly critical of an exaggerated pietism. Such men as Jean La Badie, Eberhard Gruber, Johann Conrad Beissal, Johann Kelpius and George Rapp, all of whom organized separatistic religious communities, belong more to radical Pietism.

If we would include within Pietism the kindred movements of Puritanism and Evangelicalism many other persons could be mentioned. Among those who belong more or less to the original Puritan movement are Richard Baxter, William Ames, Jeremy Taylor, John Owen, Lewis Bayly, John Robinson, John Bunyan, John Goodwin, Samuel Rutherford, John Cotton, Richard Sibbs, John Preston and William Perkins. In the later evangelical revivalism that followed we can point to the Wesleys, George Whitefield, Gilbert Tennent, Theodore Frelinghuysen, Jonathan Edwards, Charles Simeon, Howell Harris, William Wilberforce, William Carey, Charles Spurgeon, Bishop J. C. Ryle, Dwight L. Moody, George Mueller and John Nelson Darby. The latter two were the spiritual founders of the Plymouth Brethren. Mueller, it should be noted, was directly influenced by German Pietism, as was John Wesley. Darby had been in contact with French-Swiss Pietism.[3a] If we would include the Holiness movement, which arose in the nineteenth century, then we could add these names: Charles Finney; Andrew Murray; Hannah W. Smith; William Booth; Samuel Brengle; Joseph H. Smith, American holiness preacher; Oswald Chambers; A. B. Simpson, and A. W. Tozer. Many other names, of course, could be enumerated, including P. T. Forsyth, who also can be viewed as a product of Pietism. It is well to note that Forsyth spoke appreciatively of Spener, Francke and Jonathan Edwards, though he was critical of latter-day Pietism. His spiritual roots were probably more in English Puritanism, though he definitely stands in the wider tradition of Pietism.

Even the Jansenist and Quietist movements in seventeenth- and eighteenth-century Catholicism can be regarded as belonging to that wider spiritual awakening associated with Pietism. Pascal, who was very open to

[3a] The Plymouth Brethren or Assemblies of Brethren signify a divergence from the mainstream of evangelical Pietism in their separatism, dispensationalism and pronounced biblical literalism. Some groups within the Brethren should probably be put in the category of radical Pietism. In recent years some of the Brethren have shown a more irenic and cooperative spirit in their dealings with other Christians. The missionary zeal of the Brethren is to be admired.

Jansenism, has been appreciated much more among evangelicals than Roman Catholics. The Jansenists, like their Protestant brothers, stressed the total depravity of man, *sola gratia*, predestination and the religion of the heart. Saint-Cyran, one of the Jansenist theologians, reflects the Pietist emphasis in this remark: "The essence of piety is in the right ordering of the heart . . . in a heart living in this dependence and peace. It is not in the sacraments, not even in that of the body of Christ."[4] It is well to note that Jean La Badie, a convert from Roman Catholicism to Reformed Christianity and one of the luminaries of early Reformed Pietism, was greatly influenced by the Jansenist spirituality of Port Royal.[5]

In this chapter we shall use the term Pietism in its broad sense, and therefore we shall take into account the kindred movements of Puritanism and Evangelicalism. We shall not include Reformation theology, though this proved to be the seedbed of Pietism, nor Protestant scholastic orthodoxy, which was inimical to Pietism. Neither do we include such contemporary evangelical movements as the Pentecostals, which are the offspring of Pietism. We shall often be referring only to the original movement of Pietism, which it is more appropriate to call classical Pietism, but even then the theological and spiritual emphases prove remarkably similar to those of the Puritans and Evangelicals. Spener, it should be noted, was indebted to Pietistic Puritans including Lewis Bayly, author of *Practice of Piety*. Puritanism was in turn influenced by continental Pietism, and both movements left their imprint on early Methodism and later Evangelicalism. This is not to discount the different nuances in these various movements, but in discussing the legacy of Pietism we need to understand what all these have in common.

[4] See Pierre Pourrat, *Christian Spirituality*. Trans. Donald Attwater (Westminster, Maryland: Newman, 1955), p. 26.

[5] See F. Ernest Stoeffler, *The Rise of Evangelical Pietism* (Leiden: E. J. Brill, 1965), pp. 162f.

Salient Features

Among the salient features of Pietism is the emphasis upon the religion of the heart (*Herzensreligion*). The heart here refers to the center or core of the personality. In the Pietist movement there is an existential emphasis, a call for personal involvement in the truth of faith. For the Pietist faith is inward, experiential, and total. The more biblically oriented Pietists would be the first to contend that experience is not the source of faith but instead the Word of God. Yet there can be no faith apart from an experience of the heart.

Against the defenders of a creedalistic orthodoxy the Pietists like Spener and Francke insisted that faith is not just outward or intellectual: it must affect the center of one's being. For William Ames, one of the first theologians of Reformed Pietism, "Faith is the resting of the heart in God." Tersteegen held that "not in the head but in the heart is there revealed that pure and true understanding whereby we may know God and the things of God."[6] Jonathan Edwards distinguished between a speculative faith and a saving faith. The latter consists not only in "the assent of the understanding" but also in "the consent of the heart." "For," he explained, "although to true religion there must indeed be something else besides affection, yet true religion consists so much in the affections that there can be no true religion without them."[7] Whitefield was insistent that one should always preach a "felt Christ." That our very salvation is conditional upon the personal experience of the heart is attested by Carl Olaf Rosenius, nineteenth-century Swedish Pietist: "When the heart has no experience of the power of the law to its abasement, the Gospel also remains ineffective;

[6] Quoted in Walter Nigg, *Great Saints*. Trans. Wm. Stirling (Hinsdale, Ill.: Regnery, 1948), p. 224.

[7] Jonathan Edwards, *Religious Affections* (Grand Rapids: Sovereign Grace, 1971), p. 30.

Christ with all His merit remains ineffective. . . . when both Law and Gospel . . . no longer exert any influence upon the human heart, the soul is hopelessly lost."[8]

This emphasis in Pietism is already anticipated in the Old Testament. In Ezekiel we read: " 'All my words that I shall speak to you receive in your heart, and hear with your ears' " (3:10; cf. 36:26). The Psalmist prays that the Lord may create within him "a clean heart" (Ps. 51:10). Proverbs urges us to trust in the Lord with all our heart and not to rely on our understanding (3:5).

A similar note is to be found in the New Testament. Jesus said that we should believe in Him and love Him with all our heart, soul and strength (Mk. 12:30, 33). Paul contended that in addition to confessing Christ with our lips, we must believe in Him with our heart (Rom. 10:9). We can likewise point to the Johannine writings, especially I John 2:8 (NEB): "Christ has made this true, and it is true in your own experience."

This brings us to the doctrine of the new birth, which came to be a prominent theme in Pietism. While the Reformers, particularly Luther, had placed the accent on forensic justification, the Pietists spoke of the need for regeneration and sanctification. The early Pietists did not stress the experience of the new birth but the fact of the new birth. It is well to note that both Spener and Zinzendorf did not claim a special datable experience of conversion. Yet in their thought too the experiential element was not lacking. Zinzendorf declared that every individual should experience the Savior himself and not merely repeat what he has heard from his neighbor. A specific datable experience of conversion loomed much more significant in August Francke as well as in Wesley and Anglo-Saxon Evangelicalism.

While holding to the experience of the new birth the Pietists were generally distrustful of all forms of religious

[8] Carl Olaf Rosenius, *A Faithful Guide to Peace with God* (Minneapolis: Augsburg, 1923), pp. 18, 19.

enthusiasm. Religious enthusiasm might be defined as a
rapturous state of devotion born out of a crisis experience and based on the belief that one can be totally
possessed by God in the here and now. The word literally
means "in God" (*en theos*). According to Ronald Knox
in his book *Enthusiasm*, the hallmark of religious enthusiasm is the belief that nature is replaced by grace in the
redeemed. There is in the circles of religious enthusiasm a
marked openness to raptures, visions and special revelations.

The mainstream of Pietism sought to test the spirits by
the Word. Our dependence should be on the promises of
Scripture rather than on special feelings or visions. Spener
held that true belief is not so much felt emotionally as it
is known in fruits of love and obedience to God. Our
glory is in following Christ and not in feelings of rapture.
According to Francke, "Love is constant and unchanging,
and is to be discovered by your obedience to God, and
your patience under trials, rather than by your feelings."[9] Jonathan Edwards exclaimed: "For my part, I
had rather enjoy the sweet influences of the Spirit showing Christ's spiritual divine beauty, infinite grace and
dying love, drawing forth the holy exercises of faith,
divine love, sweet complacence, and humble joy in God,
one quarter of an hour, than to have prophetical visions
and revelations the whole year."[10] For Edwards the
evidence of being in the Spirit is "Christian practice."
John Wesley was also wary of religious enthusiasm, but
like Edwards he did not discount the legitimacy of special
or extraordinary experiences of God, the mystical phenomena associated with the passion of faith. Wesley held
up the ideal of Christian perfection, but in his mind this
did not mean a complete transcendence of sin but whole-
hearted commitment to Christ in love. The Anglican
evangelical, Bishop Ryle, also warned against enthusiasm:

[9] Dale W. Brown, "The Problem of Subjectivism in Pietism" (Unpub-
lished doctoral thesis; Northwestern Univ., 1962), p. 261.

[10] Jonathan Edwards, *The Works of President Edwards*, Vol. III, p. 606.

"I know no state of soul more dangerous than to imagine we are born again and sanctified by the Holy Ghost, because we have picked up a few religious feelings."[11] In the circles of radical Pietism much more emphasis was placed on extraordinary gifts and experiences.

Another distinctive theme in Pietism is the new life in Christ. While the orthodox party was primarily concerned about right doctrine, the Pietists sounded the call to sanctification, Christian perfection, spiritual and ethical obedience. It was their conviction that the Protestant Reformation remains unfulfilled unless a reform occurs in life as well as in doctrine. And this means separation from the world and holiness in thought and action. For the Pietists the Christian life is the fruit and evidence but not the basis for justification.

The assurance of salvation likewise came to occupy the attention of the Pietists. They generally believed that such assurance is conditional on obedience. Spener held that we can know we are reborn "not by a special direct revelation but by the witness of the fruit, that we obey his commands." Edwards declared: "Assurance is not to be obtained so much by self-examination, as by action." It is gained chiefly as one pushes ahead in Christian practice: "seeking and serving God with the utmost diligence is the way to have assurance and to have it maintained." In Wesley's theology assurance is given in a definite experience normally subsequent to conversion.

Pietism constantly skirted the heresy of perfectionism, and yet for the most part it did not lose sight of man's sinfulness and constant need for God's grace. Spener affirmed that though we cannot perfectly fulfill the law, by the power of the indwelling Spirit we can keep the law. He also averred: "Even if we shall never in this life achieve such a degree of perfection that nothing should be added, we are nevertheless under obligation to achieve some degree of perfection." Francke contended that "we

11 J. C. Ryle, *Holiness* (London: James Clarke, 1956), p. 25.

are perfect through Christ and in Christ through justification and imputation of the righteousness of Jesus Christ.
However, we are not and never will be entirely perfect. . . ."[12] Wesley's emphasis was on a perfection in
intention, not a sinless or absolute perfection (though he
sometimes affirmed "sinless perfection" in a very special-
ized sense). He acknowledged that the Christian could
never be free of involuntary transgressions and therefore
always needed to pray, "Forgive us our trespasses." Wesley once made the distinction between having sin and
doing sin, and sin in the latter sense can definitely be
overcome by the Christian.

Edwards diverged from the Reformation when he included love as a part of faith. Yet when he spoke of love
as the principle or foundation of faith he always had in
mind God's love. The exercise of love he regarded as an
indispensable fruit of faith. The human act of love for
Edwards may refer either to that affective, volitional
adherence to God or to working love, the love that arises
from but is potentially included in every act of faith. In
his view love is not merely the fruit of faith but belongs
to the very essence of faith. The practical consequences
of this position are that the Christian life becomes very
significant in the doctrine of salvation.

Religion and ethics are inseparable in Pietism. In the
words of John Robinson, seventeenth-century Puritan:
"God dislikes church religion which is not accompanied
in the house and streets with loving kindness and mercy
toward men." The American Reformed Pietist Theodore
Frelinghuysen, seeking to qualify certain emphases in
Calvinist orthodoxy, declared: "In the day of judgment
God will not deal with men according to election or
reprobation but according to their obedience and devout-
ness."[13]

[12] Quoted in D. Gustav Kramer, *August Hermann Francke: Ein Lebens-
bild*, I (Halle: Waisenhaus, 1880-82), p. 274.

[13] Theodorus Jacobus Frelinghuysen, *Een bunkelken leer-redenen*
(Amsterdam, 1736), pp. 19, 20. Quoted in James Tanis, "The Heidelberg

That the Pietist emphasis on the new life in Christ had decided cultural and social implications is now acknowledged by many scholars. Hans Küng maintains that witch-hunts and the burning of witches came to an end in the eighteenth century in no small part through the influence of Pietism. According to the historian William Lecky the Wesleyan revival saved England from the violent revolution that shook France. The revivals in Norway in the nineteenth century are reputed to have safeguarded morality and stability of family life there. These revivals for the most part took place within the church, unlike the situation in Sweden. Secular theologians like Gibson Winter who draw a contrast between "Pietism" and "Servanthood" simply lack historical knowledge.

Surely we need also to give attention to the deep pessimism of the Pietists concerning the capacity of reason to fathom the mysteries of God. Here the Pietists stood in basic continuity with the Reformers, though their position was clearly different in this respect from many of the leading thinkers of Protestant orthodoxy. Zinzendorf exclaimed: "He who wishes to comprehend God with his mind becomes an atheist." The Baptist Pietist, Isaac Backus, sounded a similar note: "Nothing is more certain than this, that a God which a creature can comprehend is an idol."[14] Tersteegen held that "we can never find God and truth through the activity of the mind, but through the heart and through love."[15]

Like the Reformers the Pietists recognized that man is separated from God not only by ontological fate but also by historical guilt. Both his creatureliness and sinfulness prevent him from grasping the truth about God and himself. The Pietists did not deny a natural knowledge of

Catechism in the Hands of the Calvinistic Pietists" in *Reformed Review*, Vol. 24, No. 3 (Spring, 1971), p. 156.

[14] William G. McLoughlin, *Isaac Backus and the American Pietistic Tradition* (Boston: Little, Brown, 1967), p. 172.

[15] Nigg, *op. cit.*, p. 224.

d, but for the most part they held that this is sufficient only to condemn, not to save us.

This pessimistic outlook on the capacity of reason and the senses to lead men to truth is reflected in the much beloved hymn by Tobias Clausnitzer, "Blessed Jesus at Thy Word," written in 1663:

> All our knowledge, sense and sight
> Lie in deepest darkness shrouded
> Till Thy Spirit breaks our night
> With the beams of truth unclouded.
> Thou alone to God canst win us:
> Thou must work all good within us.

The idea of the preparation of the heart for receiving Christ was also present in Pietism. In Spener's view: "It does sometimes occur . . . that God, by means of outward opportunity or inner emotion, makes the inner conscience of a man active and partially prepares him for easier acceptance of the Word."[16] This theologian held that faith is usually given instantaneously through the hearing of the Word. The idea of the prepared heart was especially prevalent in Puritanism.[17]

Though this concept can be detected in the writings of the Reformers, it was developed and expanded in Pietism. It is closely associated with the idea that the law comes before the gospel. Francke emphasized the struggle toward repentance (*Busskampf*) which is the precondition for saving faith. In Puritanism the idea of a seeking for salvation prior to faith was much in fashion.

Some of the Pietists verged towards synergism in their view that man can do something prior to his salvation. At the same time most of them were insistent that man's seeking and striving prior to grace is itself made possible by the work of the Holy Spirit. Wesley posited a pre-

[16] Philip Jacob Spener, *Theologische Bedenken*. Ed. F. A. C. Hennicke (Halle: Gebauersche Buchhandlung, 1838), p. 21.

[17] See Norman Pettit, *The Heart Prepared: Grace and Conversion in Puritan Spiritual Life* (New Haven: Yale Univ. Press, 1966).

venient grace that enabled men to prepare themselves for
the grace of salvation. The distinction was also made in
Puritan and Evangelical circles between legal repentance
and evangelical repentance; only the latter is sufficient
for salvation.

The same moral dualism that characterized the theology of the Reformation was present in Pietism. The
Pietists saw a definite dichotomy between faith and unbelief, salvation and sin, the law and the gospel, heaven
and hell, the kingdom of God and the kingdom of darkness. They had a poignant perception of the reality of the
adversary of God and man, the devil. They saw the world
as a battleground between the two kingdoms, as is evident in John Bunyan's *The Holy War*. This idea was
anticipated by the Reformers, who spoke of the "kingdom of Satan." It is also to be found in P. T. Forsyth in
his conception of the kingdom of evil. These two kingdoms were not church and state but the kingdoms of
light and darkness. The idea persisted, however, that the
state belongs basically to the domain of the kingdom of
darkness.

The Pietists differed in their conception of the demonic kingdom from Karl Barth, who sees this as essentially a
shadow-kingdom. But for Pietism the devil is not a phan-
tom of the mind nor the power of falsehood but a
personal supernatural being with real objective power. He
has been mortally wounded by the cross and resurrection
victory of Jesus Christ, but by this very fact he has
become all the more virulent.

Their stress on the spirit over the letter of the Bible is
still another salient mark of their religion. The Pietists
affirmed the infallibility of the Bible, but they were
prone to distinguish the divine content from its culturally
conditioned form. The criterion for truth is not the Bible
simply by itself but the Bible illumined by the Spirit.
They were therefore not rigid biblicists.

For Philip Spener the authority of the Bible is a
spiritual one. The biblical word is dead apart from the

testimony of the Holy Spirit. Spener also opposed a dictation theory of inspiration. "We need not think," he said, "that the Holy Spirit Himself or through an angel had to speak words to the writers or to dictate them, but He gave them divine truth through an inner enlightenment of the heart."[18] Spener also distinguished between the kernel and the husk of the Bible, between its outer and inner character.

Zinzendorf went further in acknowledging the limitations of Jesus. He said that as a child Jesus learned from the Bible much rabbinic rubbish as well as truth, but by the indwelling Spirit he forgot the error and remembered only the truth. Zinzendorf also held that the Bible sometimes erred in extraneous details such as chronology.

Johann Albrecht Bengel (1687-1752) was one of the pioneers in biblical criticism. With him begins the scientific study of the Bible text. If a text was not supported by early manuscripts he felt free to dismiss it as part of the authentic New Testament. He also held to a dynamic view of inspiration: "Scripture was divinely inspired not merely while it was being written, God breathing through the writers, but also while it is being read (and expounded), God breathing through the Scripture." The concept of the inscripturation of God's Word did not appear until much later, and while it tends to reduce revelation to a static deposit of truth, it is a poignant reminder that Scripture has a divine as well as a human authorship.

Johann Semler (1725-1791), who taught at the University of Halle, insisted that the biblical scholars wrote out of their own historical background. He also refused to affirm that all Scripture is equally inspired and held to various levels of inspiration. Like many of the neo-orthodox in the twentieth century Semler distinguished between the Bible and the Word of God. It should be noted

18 Brown, *op. cit.,* p. 211.

that in some of his liberal views he diverges from the mainstream of evangelical Pietism.

The Swedish Covenanter, Nils W. Lund (1885-1954), shared in a qualified "critical approach" to the Bible. His credentials as a Pietist, one who is fully committed to the message and life of Christ, are unassailable. Yet he assumed many of the positions of critical scholars toward Scripture including multiple sources for the Pentateuch and the Gospels, a Second Isaiah and a second-century date for Daniel.

The Pietists were attacked by the orthodox party for holding that Holy Scripture is only an outward signpost to Christ. One of the bitterest opponents of Pietism was the Lutheran V. C. Löscher, who contended that in the Bible there are no errors of any kind—physical, chronological or genealogical. The Pietists held to the full inspiration of Scripture, but their emphasis was on the inspiration of the writers, not just the words.

In English Puritanism too, questions were raised concerning the nature of the authority of Scripture. Richard Baxter admitted certain distinctions in Scripture, between the doctrine and the words that express it. John Goodwin contended that the foundation of the Christian religion is not any book or books but "those gracious counsels of God concerning the salvation of the world by Jesus Christ" which are represented and declared in Scripture. P. T. Forsyth, a modern descendant of Puritanism, held that the Bible is included in the Word of God but refused to posit a direct identity between them. In his view the true interpreter of Scripture is the evangelical experience of an awakened heart.

Joseph H. Smith, noted evangelical holiness preacher, also cautiously distinguished between the Word of God and the Scriptures. Delbert Rose interprets Smith's position as follows: "Having the *body* of Scripture without the Spirit who inspired them is to be without the Word of God. To have the Word of God one must have both the letter of Scripture and the living Spirit illuminating that letter to the believing mind."[19]

The temptation that beset Pietism was spiritualism, an appeal to the inward experience over the external Word. Yet this temptation was recognized by the guiding lights of this movement, who sought to guard against it. John Bunyan, who appealed to the testimony of the heart, nevertheless questioned this as the sole or final criterion. In his noted *Pilgrim's Progress*, "Ignorance," who based his case on the inner testimony of the heart, is asked by "Pilgrim" how he knows that he has a good heart.

With the Reformers the Pietists had a high regard for the proclaimed Word, but they became noted for their admonitions against the exhibition of scholarship and erudition in preaching. According to Spener "the pulpit is not the place for an ostentatious display of one's skill. It is rather the place to preach the Word of the Lord plainly but powerfully."[20] Oswald Chambers held that the "real fasting of the preacher is not from food, but rather from eloquence, from impressiveness and exquisite diction, from everything that might hinder the gospel of God being presented."[21] While the sermons in conventional orthodoxy were often dull and abstruse exercises in doctrinal controversies, the Pietists dealt with the realities of religious experience—the sense of sin, the yearning for salvation and the hope of God's love and mercy. George Whitefield said that "the reason why congregations have been so dead is because dead men preach to them." The Pietists stressed preaching in the power of the Spirit and in the language of the common people. Unfortunately their use of the vernacular sometimes bordered on the vulgar, but they were simply trying to follow Paul's

[19] Delbert Rose, *A Theology of Christian Experience* (Minneapolis, Minn.: Bethany, 1965), p. 145.

[20] Philip Jacob Spener, *Pia Desideria*, p. 116.

[21] Oswald Chambers, *My Utmost for His Highest*, p. 199.

example of becoming all things to all men in order to save them (I Cor. 9:22).

It is appropriate now to consider their strong emphasis on missions. Indeed, it can be said that Protestant missions began with Pietism. The Reformers did not generally concern themselves with the missionary mandate, and some of the more rigid Calvinists argued against missions on the basis that only a few belong to the elect. Zinzendorf reflected this missionary concern in his motto: "My joy until I die: to win souls for the Lamb."

The Pietists emphasized missionary training and education for missions. The Herrnhut community of Zinzendorf was the mother house of Moravian missions. Virtually all the early missionary societies within Protestantism were inspired by the evangelical awakenings. The famed Halle-Danish Mission was the product of German Pietism. Coming somewhat later were the London Missionary Society, the Wesleyan Methodist Missionary Society, the Leipzig Evangelical Lutheran Mission, the Basel Evangelical Missionary Society, the Rhenish Missionary Society, the China Inland Mission (now the Overseas Missionary Fellowship) and the Sudan Interior Mission. The Inner Mission in the nineteenth and twentieth centuries focused upon the evangelizing of the nominally Christian West. In this connection we should mention the St. Chrischona Pilgrim Mission in Basel and the Church Army in England and Denmark.

The stress upon the Christian family is also associated with Pietism. Jonathan Edwards averred that the Christian family should be a "little church." Much attention was given to family devotions and to the family altar. The Christian home was seen as both a house of hospitality and a missionary training center. William Booth, founder of the Salvation Army, put it this way:

> Every home should . . . have rules as to hours for meals, the times for prayer, the hour for rising in the morning and for retiring at night, and other similar matters. Every member of

the household should be made to cheerfully accept and honestly try to keep these rules, the spirit of loving obedience being the most important matter of all.[22]

Marriage was seen as a covenantal partnership in the Lord's service. While the Reformers relegated marriage to the order of nature, the Pietists saw Christian marriage as belonging to the order of grace as well. Zinzendorf regarded his marriage to Countess Erdmuth as a new departure in kingdom service: its purpose was said to be "gaining souls for Christ."

The priesthood of believers, though having a prominent place in the theology of the Reformers, was given concrete embodiment in Pietism. Spener advocated the formation of conventicles, private gatherings that usually met on Sunday evenings; here the sermon could be discussed, the Bible read and prayers offered. They came to be known as the *collegia pietatis*, from which the Pietist movement derives its name. As the conventicles took form, portions of devotional works were also read and discussed. Later meditations and occasionally even sermons were given as a supplement to the morning homily. Hymns and other spiritual songs were often sung at these meetings. The conventicles gave laymen an opportunity to question and test the teachings of their pastors. In the conventicle or house gathering the pastor could be called to defend his ideas and explain those which were obscure. The *collegia pietatis* provided an opportunity for worship, instruction, fellowship and mutual edification.

Spener voiced the need for the special ministry to be supplemented by the universal priesthood:

No damage will be done to the ministry by a proper use of this priesthood. In fact, one of the reasons why the ministry cannot accomplish all that it ought is that it is too weak without the help of the universal priesthood. One man is incapable of doing all that is necessary for the edification of

[22] William Booth, *The Founder Speaks Again* (London: Salvationist Publishing and Supplies, 1960), p. 124.

the many persons who are generally entrusted to his pastoral care. However, if the priests do their duty, the minister, as director and oldest brother, has splendid assistance in the performance of his duties and his public and private acts, and thus his burden will not be too heavy.[23]

While very Protestant in their espousal of the priest-hood of believers, the Pietists were also remarkably open to Catholic concerns and insights. The symbol of the ladder to heaven and the mystical idea of steps to salvation reappeared in Pietism and Puritanism. In his *The Beatitudes* Thomas Watson, seventeenth-century Puritan, rector of St. Stephen's, Wallbrook, London, presents "eight steps leading to true blessedness. They may be compared to Jacob's ladder, the top whereof reached to heaven." Others who made use of the concept of the "spiritual ladder" were Jean Taffin, Godefridus Udemans and Willem Tellinck.

Again their emphasis on the spiritual disciplines, such as meditation, early rising, protracted prayer, silence and fasting, reflects a Catholic concern. Ascetical exercises should be practiced, the Pietists believed, not to gain merit or special favor in the sight of God but to be better equipped for kingdom service.

The high view of the sacraments held by many Pietists likewise points to an affinity with Catholicism. Spener and Wesley to a lesser degree both affirmed baptismal regeneration. It can be said that the Puritans had a higher view of the Eucharistic presence than the mainline Anglicans in the seventeenth century; they even sought to bar the ignorant, the irreverent and the scandalous from Communion. At the same time Communion was celebrated infrequently in Puritan churches, and their stress on the immediacy of the Word tended to obscure the mediate role of the church and sacraments. Wesley definitely had a high view of the Eucharist. The Methodists in his lifetime far exceeded the general Anglican practice of

23 Spener, *Pia Desideria*, pp. 94, 95.

three or four communions a year. The Eucharist was also
seen as highly significant by early American evangelicals.
Some of the first great revivals were associated with
preparations for Holy Communion.

The Pietists also emphasized the importance of confirmation with special emphasis on catechetical instruction and personal dedication. Confirmation has even been
called "the child of Pietism." It is not enough to be
baptized as an infant; one must profess the faith publicly
for himself and in the presence of the congregation.
Another strand of Pietism placed the emphasis on
"believer's baptism" instead of Confirmation. In this
connection we can mention the Baptists and the Church
of the Brethren.

An appreciation of the saints is still another evidence
of openness to Catholicism. The Reformers talked
much of a "holy gospel" and "holy faith" but very little
of "holy persons." Foxe's *Book of Martyrs* became very
popular among the Puritans and Evangelicals, though it
concerned Protestant martyrs mainly. Yet there was
among the Pietists a marked appreciation for Roman
Catholic saints and mystics as well, including Augustine,
Bernard of Clairvaux, Tauler, Thomas à Kempis and the
author of *Theologia Germanica*. A. W. Tozer, modern
evangelical luminary, regards the writings of the mystics
as the single most powerful aid to his faith after the Bible
itself.

Finally we should mention the concern of many of the
Pietists for religious communities. Among the daring ventures in the communal life that were spawned by Pietism
were Herrnhut, Marienborn and the Pilgrim's Cottage in
Germany; Little Gidding and Trevecca in Britain; Ephrata
and Amana in America; the Dohnaver Fellowship in India, founded by Amy Carmichael; and the many deaconess houses in Europe and America. In our day we might
mention the Convent of the Sisters of Mary in Darmstadt,
Germany; the Brotherhood of Christ in Selbitz, Germany;

Lee Abbey and Scargill in England; and L'Abri Fellow-ship in Switzerland.

This brings us to the ecumenical thrust of Pietism. The Pietists were quick to seek spiritual unity with other Christians. For this reason they were criticized by ortho-dox confessionalists, whether Lutheran or Reformed. Spener was attacked for holding that the Evangelical (Lutheran) Church is not without error. Though anti-Catholic, Spener sought to reconcile Lutherans and Reformed. Zinzendorf held that denominations have only a relative validity. He saw that friendly cooperation is not a substitute for unity. He is reported to have had corre-spondence with the pope on a hymnbook for all Chris-tians. His Moravian missionaries did not try to build up their own denomination but simply to spread the gospel. Jonathan Edwards gave firm support to the idea of a group of Scottish ministers for a weekly interdenomina-tional and international "concern for prayer" for evange-lism and missions. In the nineteenth century J. H. Geiger proposed a visible Catholic-Evangelical church that would supersede the modernism of official Protestantism and the superstition of Rome. The Protestant deaconess com-munities sought to learn from the Catholic sisterhoods, and bonds of fellowship were forged between the sisters of both churches.

Richard Baxter voiced the irenic spirit that character-ized Pietism and Puritanism:

> I would . . . recommend to all my brethren, as the most necessary thing to the Church's peace, that they unite in necessary truths, and bear with one another in things that may be borne with; and do not make a larger creed and more necessaries than God hath done. . . . He that shall live to that happy time when God will heal His broken Churches, will see all this that I am pleading for reduced to practice, and this moderation take place of the new-dividing zeal, and the doctrine of the sufficiency of Scripture established; and all men's confessions and comments valued only as subservient

helps, and not made the test of church communion, any further than they are the same with Scripture.[24]

For Baxter as for many other Pietists and evangelicals faith should be witnessed to by word and life but not forced on people. The important thing, he said, is not to be Protestant or Catholic but Christian.

Social Dimensions of Pietism

John Hurst in his *History of Rationalism* maintains that Pietism "was aggressive not contemplative; it was practical rather than theological."[25] Perhaps he is overstating the case, since theology was not neglected, at least in early Pietism. Yet it is true that for the Pietists all theology must have practical or ethical implications. Spener held that Christians are to be God's servants in their daily work and life and that they should "prove in such service their obedience to God and their love to their fellowman." A concern for social amelioration, Francke insisted, is the indispensable fruit of conversion.

The Pietist movement was first directed to Christ and then to the world. The inner world of devotion was held in balance with the outer world of service. Perhaps not enough attention was given to the intellectual world of rational thought, but, as Kierkegaard has put it, "the highest is not to think the highest but to act upon it."

Though Spener's social approach to the world had negative overtones, it cannot be denied that he was gripped by an intense social concern. He publicly criticized the theater, dancing and card-playing on the grounds that all this was a poor stewardship of time. He also was outspoken in his denunciation of drunkenness

---

[24] Richard Baxter, *The Reformed Pastor*. Ed. Hugh Martin (Richmond: John Knox, 1956), pp. 101, 102.

[25] John F. Hurst, *History of Rationalism* (N.Y.: Charles Scribner's Sons, 1968), p. 86.

and dishonest business practices, which he regarded as a national sin.

On the positive side he stimulated a new enthusiasm for social work. Partly under his influence a workhouse was founded in Frankfurt and soon thereafter in Nürnberg, Augsburg, Leipzig, Halle and Berlin. These houses were to serve impoverished and unemployed people and also were utilized for the development of new manufactures. In addition they were often used for the housing and schooling of orphans.

August Francke is noted for his deep social conscience. He was instrumental in the founding of a house for unmarried women, an orphanage, a home for itinerant beggars, a hospital and dispensary, a widows' house and a home for needy students. He also organized services to the blind, the deaf, the dumb and the mentally ill. In addition he helped to establish a Bible society, printing presses, a missionary society and a school for poor children. Francke's attitude toward social responsibility has been characterized in this way: "Conversion and regeneration should lead man into service on behalf of the social betterment of the world."[26]

Out of German and Swiss Reformed and Lutheran Pietism emerged a host of new institutions designed to alleviate the plight of the forsaken and the poor: epileptic homes, hospitals, homes for unwed mothers, orphanages, homes for the mentally retarded and deaconess houses. The Pietists were also responsible for educational institutions, pioneering literacy programs and medical missions.

Pietism in its earlier phases placed a qualified trust in the princes and rulers to effect social justice. At the same time the leaders of this movement were not hesitant in calling upon the rulers to apply the divine mandate to the social arena. Francke was bolder in this respect than Spener and on occasion chastised the rulers from the

26 Erich Beyreuther, *August Hermann Francke* (Marburg: Francke-Buchhandlung, 1956), p. 181.

pulpit. Many of the later Pietists viewed the state with
skepticism, tending to stress its secular nature and its
unfitness to guide the moral and religious life. In general
Pietism held that it is the task of the church to give
religious and moral instruction and by its preaching of
the law of God to arouse the conscience of people,
including the secular authorities. Yet the church must
recognize that the task of administering justice belongs to
the state, and that the most it can be is a moral guide for
those who hold responsible positions in government.

The Puritans were more overtly political in that they
sought to bring direct pressure upon the state to safe-
guard public morality and promote public worship. Their
aim was to create holy commonwealths in which every
area of life would be directly under the revealed law of
God. This reflects Calvin's ideal of the "holy community," which was realized partly in the city-state of
Geneva. Yet neither Calvin nor the Puritans sought a
theocracy, for church and state still had their own distinctive duties.

John Howard Yoder, noted Mennonite scholar, has
made this trenchant observation:

> It is certainly not the case that pietism, whether we think
> now of the eighteenth century movement or of its more
> recent spiritual heirs, was uninterested in social or political
> ethics. Few movements in church history and few schools of
> theological conviction have been, in proportion to popula-
> tion, so productive of institutional inventiveness and cultural
> creativity as have been the Moravians, the Methodists, and
> their counterparts within the larger churches.[27]

Yoder goes on to say that when the Pietists raised the
cry, "Keep the church out of politics," they did not
mean that politics is out of bounds for the Christian but
that the church hierarchy (the clerics) should not inter-
fere with lay Christians who entered politics as their

[27] John Howard Yoder, *The Christian Witness to the State* (Newton,
Kansas: Faith and Life, 1964), p. 85.

vocation. Also we might add that they did not want to confuse the gospel with a political platform or social ideology.

Both social service and political action have been prominent in later Pietism (Evangelicalism). The Clapham sect in England, which was composed of wealthy Evangelical laymen, was instrumental in the abolition of the slave traffic. William Wilberforce, an Evangelical member of Parliament, was an influential and vigorous leader in the crusade against slavery. One of the most popular evangelical treatises of the time was his *Practical View of the Prevailing Religious System of Professed Christians in the Higher and Middle Classes in this Country Contrasted with Real Christianity*.

John Wesley, who preached the gospel of regeneration, sought to demonstrate the fruits of the new birth in his daily life. Besides working for the abolition of slavery he instituted clinics and credit unions. He held that the increase of personal wealth is the most subtle foe to a life of consecration. In a pamphlet entitled *Thoughts on the Present Scarcity of Provisions* he expressed advanced social views, including the recommendation that the breeding of cattle and sheep should be increased in order to place larger stocks of beef within reach of the poor. He also complained that there was a grave injustice in allowing one town "half the size of Islington" to send four members to Parliament while the largest county in North Wales sent only one.

Etienne De Grellet, Quaker evangelist, was instrumental in prison reform in several European countries. As a result of his efforts youths were separated from hardened criminals, and lighter irons were substituted for heavier ones. In America in his journeys to the South he protested against slavery, openly declaring that all kinds of oppression are contrary to the law of God.

John Woolman, eighteenth-century Quaker, was chiefly responsible for the eradication of the slave practice in the Quaker community in America. Whenever he

spoke at Friends meetings he would point out the iniquity of slave-keeping and urged slave-owners to give up
their slaves. He also counseled his Quaker brethren to
refuse payment of the tax that was levied for the prosecu-
tion of the French and Indian War.

Lewis Tappan was an evangelical who was active in the
abolitionist movement in America. His house was ran-
sacked and his possessions burned as a result of his
anti-slavery stand. He decried violence as a means of
correcting the situation. He also insisted that the anti-
slavery crusade be effective first within the churches.

Charles Finney, the noted revival preacher, was also
involved for a time in the abolitionist movement. Oberlin
College, over which he presided, was accused by Old
School Presbyterians of being the hotbed of "revivalism,
fanaticism and social reform." Finney took part in the
formation of the New York Anti-Slavery Society, and in
December of 1833 he banned "slave-holders and all concerned in the traffic" from communion in his New York
church. At the same time he would not treat Negroes as
social equals and at Oberlin wanted them to sit separately
from whites.

The Wesleyan Methodist Church, founded in 1843,
emphasized from the very beginning practical holiness
and humanitarianism. Adherence to its anti-slavery stand
was a condition for membership. The new church pro-
hibited slavery and intoxicating liquor.

John White, English Methodist missionary to the black
community in South Africa, championed the oppressed
among the blacks against their white exploiters. He
secured a law prohibiting the sale of liquor to natives
outside the larger towns, which completely transformed
the mine barracks. In 1908 he helped to block the con-
cession of native lands to a great meat extract company.
In 1914 he was instrumental in defeating plans for taking
over lands in the Reserve by a railway company.

Many other examples of selfless social service can be
given. Hans Nielsen Hauge, who is called the Wesley of

Norway, in addition to itinerant evangelism established a gristmill and kitchen to support himself and his charities and to feed the hungry. Josephine Butler in nineteenth-century England campaigned against licensed brothels and the state control of prostitution. John Bost, Huguenot preacher in France, saw that homes were provided for idiots, epileptics and cripples. Friedrich von Bodelschwingh established in Bielefeld in Westphalia houses for epileptics, consumptives, neurotics and alcoholics as well as hospitals for the physically ill. Eva von Winckler, Lutheran deaconess, founded and directed hospitals, orphanages and rescue homes. Phoebe Palmer, Methodist urban evangelist in America, founded in 1850 the Five Points Mission; this marked the beginning of Protestant institutional work in the slums. James Hardie, who was converted at one of Dwight L. Moody's evangelistic campaigns in Edinburgh, applied himself to the needs of the working people in Scotland and founded the British Labour Party. Abraham Kuyper, in whom Pietism and orthodoxy came together, denounced the reluctance of the Christian community to take part in public affairs and led a successful battle against secular opposition for the preservation of Christian schools in the Netherlands.

The Salvation Army should also be mentioned for its role not only in social services but in social action as well. Commander Booth-Tucker, Salvationist missionary in India, worked for the establishment of hospitals and dispensaries, for improved sanitation and for the sinking of wells. He also helped to form village banks to fight usury. General Evangeline Booth publicly attacked the owners of dilapidated slum properties in New York City who charged exorbitant rents. She also spoke out against drunkenness and lent her prestige to the prohibition movement (as did also Billy Sunday and other American evangelists). Charles Péan, Salvation Army officer in France, ministered to the prisoners on Devil's Island and through his public protests played a major role in the closing of that infamous prison.

This is not to overlook the compromises latter-day evangelicals have made with the values of bourgeois society, and yet it can be shown that there are always a few who are willing to stand against the stream. Sam Jones, American evangelist in the early twentieth century, was a pioneer in urban reform. While many other evangelical preachers at that time were telling the poor to be submissive and humble, he urged respectable churchgoers to enact laws to restrain the unconverted. Evangelicals today who simply say that belief in the gospel is the only answer to the social crisis without pressing for corrective legislation are not being true to their own tradition.

In their social concern the Pietists generally refrained from making the mistake of many in the modern Social Gospel movement of identifying the kingdom of God with the progressive movement in politics and its goal of a democratic egalitarian society. In this connection we might examine the social philosophy of Christoph Blumhardt, who was active for a time in the Socialist movement in Germany. His sensitivity to social evils is reflected in this remark: "What use is it to prattle about the kingdom of heaven if you leave your fellow men in their fetters and bonds, the slaves in their chains, and the oppressed in their misery?"[28] Blumhardt sympathized with the Marxist criticism of the inhuman exploitation of the poor, and yet he saw that our social gains and reforms would not be permanent. "The social movement as we see it today," he said, "still belongs to the world which will pass. It does not contain the fellowship of men as it will one day come through God's Spirit."[29] The messianic pretensions of the socialists would eventually subvert whatever real social progress was made. "The attempt to carry my idea of God into earthly things cannot take root

[28] R. Lejeune, ed., *Christoph Blumhardt and His Message* (Woodcrest, Rifton, N.Y.: Plough Publishing House, 1963), pp. 64, 65.

[29] *Ibid.*, p. 73.

at a time when men are filled with the hope that they and they alone can create a blissful humanity."[30]

Blumhardt asserts that we can strive for justice in this world because the principal victory over the powers of darkness has already been effected by Jesus Christ. And yet the kingdom of God will not come until God brings it in His own way and time. But in our struggles on behalf of the oppressed we must look forward in expectation to the advent of God's new order. We should not be content that only a few people are saved. We must hope and pray that on all the earth the new light will someday shine. Blumhardt saw in the ferment in the nations, the agitation of the poor and the crying out for the right to live, signs of the dawning of the new aeon. Our struggle for justice is itself a witness to the victory of Jesus Christ.

It is important to remember that social service was generally seen by the Pietists not as an end in itself but as a means to a higher end, the conversion of the whole man to the living God. In our social concern we must labor for the inward liberation of men from sin and doubt. There can be no lasting just society apart from a new kind of man. By our demonstration of Christian kindness and mercy we can plant the seeds of faith in Jesus Christ. The motivation in our social service is love, but the goal is evangelism. This dictum of St. Teresa of Avila, Roman Catholic spiritual writer and mystic, reflects the stance of evangelical Pietism: "The soul of the care of the poor is the care of the poor soul." St. Teresa and the Pietists are here being true to the example of our Lord, who fed the hungry and healed the sick, out of compassion to be sure, but with the ultimate aim of creating within them a hunger for God and a yearning for the spiritual healing that faith alone gives.

---

[30] *Ibid.*

Pietism and Mysticism

Albrecht Ritschl in his well-known *History of Pietism* maintains that the motifs of medieval mysticism reappear in Protestantism through Pietism. Pietism marks a return, in his view, to Roman Catholic concerns and values. A case could be made that Pietism admittedly has some affinities with the practical piety of the *devotio moderna* exemplified in the Brethren of the Common Life, but its relation with high mysticism is much more tenuous. Indeed, it can be shown that there are definite tensions between Pietism and the mainstream of Christian mysticism. Also one could argue with some persuasiveness that Pietism derives its chief inspiration from the Protestant Reformers, particularly Luther and Calvin. Spener quoted from Luther voluminously, and Wesley was deeply affected by Luther's *Commentary on Romans*. Nevertheless the relationship between Pietism and Catholic mysticism needs to be explored, since it cannot be doubted that the mystical dimension is very much present in Pietism.

Christian mysticism signifies a synthesis of Platonic and neo-Platonic and perhaps also Oriental strands with biblical faith. Some mystics have been much more biblical than others, while a few think primarily in Hellenistic terms. Just as there exists a tension within Christian mysticism between biblical and Hellenistic motifs so in Pietism there is a tension between mystical and Reformation motifs.

One of the hallmarks of mysticism is a direct experience of God. In the view of the Pietists we have a direct experience of God but only in Christ. Our experience is made possible because of the Mediator between God and man. And it is generally in conjunction with the written or spoken Word. Robert Barclay, the Quaker mystic, stands much closer to mysticism and radical Pietism than to evangelical Pietism in his *Apology* (Prop. II): "These divine inward revelations . . . are not to be subjected to the test either of the outward testimony of the Scripture or of the natural reason of man. . . . for this divine revelation and inward illumination is that which is evident and clear of itself." Joachim Lange, a colleague of Francke, better reflects the general stance of Pietism: "Not the immediate revelation, but the written, read, preached, and examined Word of God has been the regular means to calling, conversion, and salvation."[31] Both Spener and Francke allowed for the possibility of direct special revelations apart from the Bible, but these must be in conformity to Scripture.

Again God is the Agent as well as the Subject for the mainstream of Pietism. God's mighty acts in history and the work of the Holy Spirit within are equally important. It is interesting to note that the term *Heilsgeschichte* (history of salvation) was first used in the circles associated with Bengel.[32] Nevertheless, in Pietism the historical basis has sometimes been pushed into the background, and the really important thing is the birth of God in the soul of man. This tendency reflects a definite affinity with the Catholic mystical tradition.

Both the Catholic mystics and the Pietists spoke of Christ as the Savior from sin as well as the example or pattern for life. At the same time the emphasis is often placed on the latter rather than the former. Johann Arndt, Lutheran mystic and proto-Pietist, reminded his hearers of the sacred obligation that is laid upon the Christian to bear the cross after the example of Christ. "This denying self, bearing Christ's cross, following Christ . . . this is . . . the sufficient highest honor for which we are to strive."[33] Against the subtle emphasis on

[31] Brown, *op. cit.*, pp. 216, 217.

[32] See Otto Piper, *"Heilsgeschichte"* in Marvin Halverson, ed., *A Handbook of Christian Theology* (N.Y.: Meridian, 1958) [pp. 156-159], p. 156.

[33] Johann Arndt, *Devotions and Prayers of Johann Arndt.* Trans. and ed. John J. Stoudt (Grand Rapids: Baker, 1958), p. 30. Note that Ernest Stoeffler regards Arndt and not Spener as the real father of Pietism.

works which developed in Pietism Zinzendorf and the Moravians emphasized the "blood and the Lamb," the substitutionary atonement of Christ.

The Pietists for the most part remained true to their Reformation heritage in stressing that our salvation is a product of free grace. They acknowledged that we cannot cooperate with God in procuring it, but we can cooperate in maintaining it. Some also contended that we can prepare ourselves for it, but only on the basis of prevenient grace. Man can be active before his justification but only by a preliminary work of the Holy Spirit. The mystical ideas of the "ladder to heaven," "steps to salvation" and the *unio mystica* as the last step in the *ordo salutis* (order of salvation) found their way into the spirituality of some of the early Pietists, though generally in the context of *sola gratia*.

It is interesting to note how even in the Lutheran mystic, Jacob Boehme, who is sometimes classified as a radical Pietist, the emphasis on grace gives a new cast to some of the traditional mystical concepts. For Boehme, who stressed God's initiative, Jacob's ladder was not the mystical hierarchy of states but a struggling path, the pilgrim's way of obedience made possible by grace. He wrote: "I did not climb up into the Godhead, neither can so mean a man as I am do it; but the Godhead climbed up in me and revealed such to me out of his Love. . . ."[34] Boehme's mysticism was characterized not by man's ascent to God but by God's descent to man. Biblical and Platonic motifs exist side by side in his mystical theology.

In the mainstream of evangelical Pietism justification is treated as the forensic imputation of righteousness, not as inner transformation (as, e.g., in Tauler and the *Theologia Germanica*). The Pietists like the Reformers maintained that we are justified while we are still sinners. Samuel Rutherford declared: "Stand not upon sanctification, but

[34] See John Joseph Stoudt, *Jacob Boehme* (N.Y.: Seabury, 1968), p. 61.

upon justification. Hand all your accounts over to free grace."[35]

At the same time the Pietists were adamant that justification is inseparable from regeneration and sanctification. They were insistent that justification must have concrete effects in man's life, that it must issue in sanctification. The evidence for our justification, they contended, is a holy life, though they refrained from saying that this is the condition for our justification. According to Spener, though faith alone justifies and makes holy, faith is "inseparable from good works," so no one can be justified "other than those who are intent on sanctification."[36]

When the Pietists spoke of conversion they had in mind a change from sin and death to the new life in Christ. Conversion is both an event and a lifelong struggle. Those mystics who stand more in the Platonic tradition were prone to speak of a conversion from the manifold to the essential, from the temporal to the eternal. This note is also present in radical Pietism.

For both the Catholic mystics and the Pietists the goal of the Christian life is union with God. But the Pietists were more prone to think of this as union with the will of God, not a merging into the being of God. The accent was placed on identification with the passion and victory of Christ, not identity with the essence of God. Surely this note is also to be found in the more evangelical mystics such as Bernard of Clairvaux. The Pietists maintained that we become united in fellowship with God and the saints rather than with the being of God. This is why communion and fellowship are more significant in evangelical Pietism than the concept of identity. Edwards averred that the saints are not made partakers of the essence of God but of His spiritual beauty and blessedness.

[35] Alexander Whyte, *Samuel Rutherford and Some of his Correspondents*, p. 160.

[36] Brown, *op. cit.*, p. 244.

As has been intimated, Pietism affirmed both the Bible
and the inner light, and yet the latter was generally made
subordinate to the former. The Spirit illumines the Word
but does not bring to us a new Word. Many mystics were
prone to place the inner testimony of the heart over both
the church and the Bible. Even Tersteegen, the Protestant
mystic, contended that God can and does work without
any external medium. He even wrote to the consternation
of some of his evangelical brethren: "You yourself should
become a Holy Writ." In this respect Tersteegen stands
closer to the tradition of mysticism than to Protestant
Pietism.

The more evangelical among the Pietists were exclusive
and unyielding in their adherence to the historical particularity of the biblical revelation. Mystics, on the other
hand, who appeal to a common religious experience, are
more apt to be syncretistic than separatistic. For the
mainstream of Pietism the basis for fellowship is not a
common religious experience nor a common quest for
truth, but a common faith in Jesus Christ. Christianity
was considered to be both the way to life and a way of
life. An exclusively mystical stance results in a marked
tolerance and openness. Since mysticism was present
among the Pietists they proved to be more irenic than
confessional orthodoxy. But their tolerant attitude was
aimed primarily toward other Christians, not toward pagans or infidels.

It can be said that Pietism affirmed fellowship as well
as solitude in the life of the Christian. Plotinus' mystical
"flight of the alone to the alone" was foreign to the
mainstream of Pietism. Zinzendorf held that it is "in the
nature of our religion to have companionship." Wesley
spoke for many when he said that our goal is not "holy
solitariness" but "social holiness."

At the same time the Pietists also saw the need for
periodic solitude. Men like Tersteegen, Edwards and
Richard Baxter were especially emphatic on the important role of solitude in the Christian life. In the words of

Baxter: "We are fled so far from the solitude of superstition that we have cast off the solitude of contemplative devotion. . . . We seldom read of God's appearing by himself or his angels to any of his prophets or saints in a throng, but frequently when they are alone."[37] Tersteegen, who was still more mystical, affirmed: "Solitude is the school of godliness; for this reason you must wholly shun needless intercourse with men."[38]

It is true to say that Pietism at its best sought to hold action and contemplation in balance. Like Thomas Aquinas the evangelicals affirmed the superiority of the mixed life and especially the apostolate over permanent monastic seclusion on the one hand and social activism on the other. Contemplation should serve the cause of mission just as mission will drive us ever again to contemplation. Evangelical Pietists would find difficulty with this sentiment of Thomas à Kempis: "The spiritual man puts the care of his soul before all else."[39] The first priority is the glory of God and the advancement of His kingdom.

Unlike most of the mystics the Pietists were characterized by a dualistic rather than a monistic orientation. Pure mysticism tends toward pantheism, and this tendency can be detected even among the Christian mystics. According to Eckhart the core of the soul is God. In the words of Teresa of Avila: "There is nothing in me that is not God: my 'me' is God." Catherine of Genoa, who was probably more Hellenistic than biblical in her thought, stated: "My being is God, not by simple participation but by a true transformation of my being." Some of these statements should be regarded as hyperboles, and yet they reflect a decided monistic stance. Some of the

[37] Richard Baxter, *The Saints' Everlasting Rest* (Old Tappan, N.J.: Revell, 1962), p. 150.

[38] Nigg, *op. cit.,* p. 209.

[39] Thomas a Kempis, *The Imitation of Christ.* Trans. Leo Sherley-Price (London: Penguin, 1959), p. 73.

mystics would speak of nature as the mask of God or simply as the world of appearance. This Platonic note can even be discerned in Thomas Merton: "For the 'unreality' of material things is only relative to the greater reality of spiritual things."[40] Others were inclined to conceive of the whole world as being filled with the presence and glory of God and thereby tended in the direction of theopanism.

For evangelical Pietism there are two worlds, grace and sin, and two kingdoms, that of light and darkness. In Platonic mysticism the two worlds are the temporal and the eternal, and this idea sometimes entered into Pietism. For the most part the Pietists envisioned an adversary of God who is in the world and who stands over the world. The Christian was seen as a soldier of the cross, not simply one of the enlightened or holy men. The image of the "pilgrim" was common to both Pietism and Catholic mysticism. Like the mystics the Pietists spoke of Christ dwelling within, but He was never identified with the deepest within the self, except among some of the more radical Pietists.[41]

The terrible reality of sin figured very prominently in Pietism, and sin was seen as unbelief and rebellion against God. Many of the mystics, particularly those of a more biblical orientation, also agonized over sin, and yet Platonic notions often intruded into their thinking. The mystics generally preferred to speak of the weakness and insufficiency of man rather than of his total depravity. The soul was seen as being held down by the flesh, and the goal was to gain liberation from the bonds of the flesh. The antithesis was envisioned as between nature

[40] Thomas Merton, *Thoughts in Solitude* (N.Y.: Farrar, Straus & Cudahy, 1958), pp. 17, 18.

[41] Nevertheless the leaders of Pietism sometimes came close to affirming a mystical identification of the believer and Christ. Spener once preached an advent sermon in which he remarked that the believer can say, "I am Christ," since the union between Christ and the believer is so intimate. Hans Bruns, *Philipp Jacob Spener* (Basel: Brunner-Verlag, 1955), p. 54.

and grace, whereas in evangelicalism it is between sin and grace. As evangelicals understand it, the dichotomy is not between ignorance and enlightenment (as in much of mysticism) but between sinfulness and holiness.

Again, the tensions between Pietism and mysticism can be illuminated by comparing the two kinds of love, Agape and Eros, which were ably delineated by Anders Nygren in his book of that title. According to Nygren Augustine's *Caritas,* which had a great influence on the development of Christian mysticism, was a compromise between Agape, self-giving love, and Eros, self-seeking or self-regarding love, with the Eros motif being dominant. Nygren interpreted Agape, which was spoken of in the New Testament, as the love which does not seek its own and which is not conditional on the worth of the one loved. In Eros, the dominant motif in Platonic mysticism, man seeks his own good even in the quest for God. In *Caritas* we love God as the object of our greatest need; He is our highest good apart from which we cannot find satisfaction. It is probably true to say that the Pietists combined aspects of Eros and Agape, much as did Augustine, though the Agape motif would be much more prominent than in the pure forms of mysticism. The Hellenistic conception can certainly be seen in the Puritan John Preston, who held that in spiritual love our ardor and passion are directed no longer to worldly things but to the Holy. It is well to note that in Pietism the emphasis was placed much more on self-denial than on self-realization, on self-sacrifice than on self-fulfillment.

Henry Scougal, one of the saints of Scottish Protestantism, reflects the Augustinian conception in holding that love is miserable when there is not worth enough in its object "to answer the vastness of its capacity." For Scougal as for Augustine love is not satisfied until it finds an object of eternal worth. On the other hand, the Agape motif in his thought also finds expression when he defines perfect love as "a kind of self-dereliction . . . wherein the lover dies to himself and all his own interests, not thinking of them, nor caring for them any more, and minding nothing but how he may please and gratify the party whom he loves."[42] Interestingly enough Scougal's *The Life of God in the Soul of Man* had a marked influence upon both John and Charles Wesley and George Whitefield.

Jonathan Edwards said that seeking our own happiness is not wrong so long as we seek it in God. But he also insisted that God loves us even while we are still sinners. Yet he diverges from the Reformation in his view that God has greater love for those who persist in the life of fidelity and devotion. He reflects Christian mystical motifs when he avers that "those that have been most eminent in fidelity and holiness . . . are most beloved by Christ in heaven."[43]

The mystical imprint upon the Pietists is again evident in their view that the Christian life or the holy life can be a veritable means of grace in addition to the preaching of the Word of God. Spener held that personal holiness "contributes much to conversion" of others.[44] Edwards declared: "Words are of no use any otherwise than as they convey our own ideas to others; but actions, in some cases, may do it much more fully. There is a language in actions; and in some cases, much more clear and convincing than in words."[45] And again: "If those who call themselves Christians generally walked in all the paths of virtue and holiness, it would tend more to the advancement of the Kingdom of Christ in the world . . . than all the sermons in the world."[46]

In the area of prayer the significant place assigned to

[42] Henry Scougal, *The Life of God in the Soul of Man* (London: Inter-Varsity, 1962), p. 38.

[43] Jonathan Edwards, *Christian Love and Its Fruits* (Grand Rapids: Sovereign Grace, 1971), pp. 163, 164.

[44] Spener, *Pia Desideria*, p. 102.

[45] Jonathan Edwards, *The Works of President Edwards*, Vol. III, p. 509.

[46] Ralph Trumbull, ed., *Devotions of Jonathan Edwards* (Grand Rapids: Baker, 1959), p. 32.

silence also bears the mark of a mystical orientation. Yet in the mainstream of Pietism silence is not to be used to get beyond the Word; rather it should serve to prepare men for the Word and also to induce them to reflect upon it. In the more extreme forms of mysticism the goal is to ascend above the rational into the ineffable.

Like the mystics the Pietists speak highly of the practice of meditation in the life of devotion, but the object of our meditation should not be the naked being of God (as in pure mysticism) but the mighty acts of God culminating in His gracious condescension in Jesus Christ. Our reflection should generally be focused upon the goodness and love of God, not upon the core of the soul or the ground of being. John Owen recommended frequent meditation both on "the holy excellencies of the divine nature" and on Jesus Christ as "a most useful preparation for prayer."[47]

Prayer for the Pietists includes heartfelt supplication and intercession as well as adoration and thanksgiving. Contemplative adoration was regarded as the highest form of prayer by some Pietists, and here again the mystical note is evident. For Johann Arndt inner prayer and transcendent prayer are superior to verbal prayer:

> Transcendent prayer takes place through union with God in faith where our spirit melts and sinks down into God's uncreated Spirit. What the soul there knows is inexpressible and when, in such high devotion, it is asked what it knows it answers, "A good above all goods."[48]

A similar note can be found in O. Hallesby, the Norwegian Pietist, in his noted book *Prayer*. Hallesby also spoke of a prayer without words which can carry a person through despair and the struggle of death. The real essence of prayer, as he saw it, was the right attitude of

[47] John Owen, *The Holy Spirit: His Gifts and Power* (Grand Rapids: Kregel, 1967), p. 336.

[48] Arndt, *op. cit.*, p. 72.

the heart, not verbal petition, though the latter definitely has its place.

P. T. Forsyth stands closer to the position of the Reformation by stressing the elements of petition, asking and seeking in prayer. In his view the object of prayer is to move and change God's will, for the kind of God that the Bible speaks of chooses to realize His purposes in cooperation with His children, and therefore He makes Himself at least partially dependent upon their pleadings. At the same time Forsyth assigns a prominent place to adoration, which signifies both the beginning and goal of prayer. "At the height of prayer," he wrote, "if not at its beginning, we are preoccupied with the great and glorious thing God has done for His own holy name in Redemption, apart from its immediate and particular blessing to us."[49]

It is well to observe that pure mysticism tends to deny the validity of petition and intercession. Meister Eckhart exclaimed: "People often say to me: 'Pray for me!' At that I have to wonder . . . why not be your true self and reach into your own treasure? For the whole truth is just as much in you as in me!"[50] The motto of Francis de Sales was: "Require nothing, refuse nothing." This stands in sharp contrast to evangelicals like Adolphe Monod, Spurgeon, Moody and Finney, all of whom spoke of striving with God in prayer. Instead of counseling unqualified submission or resignation to the divine order of things they sounded the call to "prevailing prayer."

For the Pietists faith is both an encounter with Christ and a participation in Christ and God. It entails not only a mystical awareness of and communion with God but also venture and trust. In addition it includes the notes of

---

49 P. T. Forsyth, *The Soul of Prayer* (Grand Rapids: Eerdmans, n.d.), p. 35.

50 Raymond Blakney, *Meister Eckhart: A Modern Translation* (N.Y.: Harper, 1941), p. 128.

certainty, assurance and confidence. The certainty of
faith, moreover, is based on the promises of Christ declared in Scripture, not on the experience of faith.

In evangelical Pietism there is an emphasis on the
holiness of God over the eternity of God, on the sovereignty of God over the beatific vision of God. For both
the Christian mystics and the Pietists the goal of life is to
glorify God, but while the mystics had in mind chiefly
spiritual works of adoration and prayer, the Pietists
placed equal emphasis upon ethical obedience. In Pietism and Puritanism God is glorified in outgoing service
to our fellowman. There is a practical orientation in
Pietism that may be contrasted with the otherworldly
character of mysticism. At the same time the Pietists
stressed that our service in this life is a preparation for
life in eternity with God. They championed an otherworldliness that gives significance to life in this world.

To do justice to Christian mysticism, the ethical note is
by no means absent. Besides speaking of a spiritual marriage between God and the soul, many of the mystics
referred to a spiritual fecundity in which we share the
fruits of our contemplation with the world. Mystics such
as Catherine of Siena, Francis of Assisi, Henry Suso,
Catherine of Genoa, Teresa of Avila and Francis Borgia
are known for their works of mercy and self-giving service. A great number of mystics are also noted for their
involvement in the political issues of their times; we can
here mention Gregory the Great, Bernard of Clairvaux,
Catherine of Siena, Teresa of Avila, Ignatius Loyola and
Nicholas of Flüe. It can be said that the biblical and
evangelical elements in Christian mysticism prevented it
from becoming overly detached and isolated from the
crying needs and concerns in the world. John Tauler
echoed the views of many of the mystics and of the
Pietists as well when he declared: "That a man should
have a life of quiet or rest in God is good; that a man
should lead a painful life in patience is better; but that a

man should have rest in a painful life is best of all!" [51]
Here we discern how mysticism at its best is in touch
with the tensions and opportunities of human life.

The spiritual affinity between Pietism and mysticism
can finally be seen in the attention given by the Pietists
to spiritual disciplines and asceticism. But for Pietism and
Puritanism this is an innerworldly asceticism, one that is
realized in fulfilling our secular vocation in society. They
also spoke of the need for an asceticism to equip one for
mission. Here we see a similarity to Ignatius Loyola and
his Society of Jesus. For the most part spiritual disciplines were viewed not as means to salvation, but as aids
in the struggle of the Christian life. They are designed to
help us accomplish specific tasks in the world.

Among the spiritual disciplines prevalent in Pietism
were early rising, Sabbath observance, fasting, protracted
prayer, the keeping of prayer lists, tithing, meditation,
silence and simplicity. George Whitefield confessed:
"Whole days and weeks have I spent prostrate on the
ground in silent or vocal prayer." J. Hudson Taylor of the
China Inland Mission would rise at 2:00 for his morning
watch and then return to bed at 4:00 a.m. Another who
was noted for his early rising for prayer was John Wesley.

Forsyth, who stands in the piety and tradition of
Puritanism, gives an apt description of the role of discipline in the Christian life: "Christianity is much harder
than any asceticism. How hard it is to be a Christian. It is
freedom, but true freedom is only possible under discipline, and the greater the aim the more discipline is
required."[52]

Pietism and Fundamentalism

Fundamentalism is a later nineteenth- and twentieth-
century movement that has its roots in Pietism as well as

[51]In Evelyn Underhill, *The Mystics of the Church* (N.Y.: Schocken,
1944), p. 142.

[52] Harry Escott, ed., *The Cure of Souls* (Grand Rapids: Eerdmans,
1948), p. 110.

in Protestant scholastic orthodoxy and the dispensation-alism of the Plymouth Brethren. Ernest Sandeen contends that it signifies the union of the Princeton School of Theology (A. A. Hodge, Charles Hodge, Warfield) and dispensationalism.[53] I think it would be more accurate to say that it represents a union of scholastic orthodoxy (both Reformed and Lutheran) and latter-day Pietism, which includes both premillennial and perfectionistic strands. Sandeen omits the perfectionism of the Holiness movement in tracing the development of fundamentalist spirituality. Within fundamentalism there exists a tension between the heritage of Pietism and a rigid confessional orthodoxy.

We do not wish to be negative in our appraisal of fundamentalism. It has been right in its concern that the supernaturalistic orientation of the Bible not be discarded in favor of the modern naturalistic world view. It has also kept alive the opposition to the secular myth of evolution that Protestant liberalism seemed to accept uncritically. Yet fundamentalism became overly defensive and hyper-sensitive. It often succumbed to the rationalistic methods of its foes, thereby confusing a theological method with the empiricist method of induction or the idealistic method of deduction. It sought to combat the modern world view on its own grounds and thereby seriously compromised the integrity of the Christian faith. At its best it preserved a fervent evangelical piety, though it was admittedly otherworldly.

While the fundamentalists were deeply concerned with assent to the truths of the faith, such as the bodily resurrection of Christ, the Virgin Birth and second coming, the Pietists gave primary attention to the Christian life. Both life and doctrine are important, but neither should be emphasized to the exclusion of the other.

---

[53] See Ernest R. Sandeen, *The Origins of Fundamentalism* (Philadelphia: Fortress, 1967); and his *The Roots of Fundamentalism* (Chicago: Univ. of Chicago Press, 1970).

Indeed, it can be said that Pietism can flourish only on the soil of orthodoxy.

Unlike modern fundamentalism the Pietists were generally loyal to the organized church. Their goal was to work within the church as a leaven. They often saw themselves as an ecclesiola within the ecclesia. In Pietism there was even a marked ecumenical thrust. Zinzendorf envisioned a single church in which Lutherans and Calvinists would be united with Catholics. A great many fundamentalists would find much difficulty with Christoph Blumhardt's sentiment: "I still have hope that Christians will be able to unite again. If our hearts are filled with His being, what does it matter whether one is Catholic or Protestant?"[54] The Pietists were generally more irenic than polemical.

In stark contrast the fundamentalists often became sectarian and separatistic. The institutional church was generally seen as apostate; this is particularly true among the dispensationalists. Here we see an affinity with radical Pietism, which advocated withdrawal from the organized church.

A marked difference can also be seen in the area of eschatology. The early Pietists and the Puritans were for the most part postmillennialists, though the premillennial and amillennial views were also represented.[55] The Christian faith was widely regarded as a leaven that would permeate the whole world. Such a position, of course, gives significance to social reform. Spener saw a new age of promise for Christianity breaking in during earthly history. Edwards spoke of "the advancement of Christ's kingdom on earth." A "holy optimism" characterized many of the early evangelicals. It is to be noted that even Hodge and Warfield were postmillennialists.

The modern fundamentalist movement has generally been premillennialist and dispensationalist. J. N. Darby's

54 Lejeune, op. cit., p. 217.
55 See Iain Murray, The Puritan Hope (London: Banner of Truth, 1971).

influence on fundamentalism has been more decisive in
this respect than that of Spener or Edwards, since Darby
denied a golden age for the church in which the gospel
would be mightily spread throughout the world; instead
he looked forward to the immediate return of Christ and
His earthly millennial reign. This kind of emphasis reflects an overly pessimistic view of both the church and
world and has led to a not surprising detachment from
political concerns, since the world is held to be incurably
evil. The presumption that we are in the last days also
tends to undercut any impetus for social reform. The goal
is not to advance the kingdom in the world but to
proclaim a kingdom that will be instituted in the not too
distant future by divine intervention. The premillennial
position nevertheless has kept alive the hope that God's
purposes will be fulfilled on earth as they are in heaven.

A divergence can also be seen in the way the two
movements approach Scripture. For men like Hodge,
Warfield and Van Til the Bible is a system of truth
yielding information about God and the world. For the
Pietists the Bible is a living testimony concerning Christ
and His offer of salvation. [55a] It is treated not so much as
a paper pope but more as a treasure of devotion. While
the fundamentalists defend the letter of Scripture and
often lapse into a biblical literalism, the Pietists were
more concerned with the spirit of the Bible. William
Booth reflects this concern:

> Great as is the value of the Bible, it is possible to exalt it
> too highly. It is sometimes put in the place of God. The
> letter of it rather than its spirit has been held in chief regard.
> Others have made the mistake of regarding it as the only
> revelation God has made to the world. It contains the fullest
> and the clearest, but not the only, light He has given to
> men. [56]

55a In E. R. Geehan, ed., *Jerusalem and Athens* (Nutley, N.J.: Presbyterian and Reformed, 1971), pp. 154-165. Jack Rogers discusses how Van
Til's position on Scripture diverges from the Westminster divines.

56 Booth, *op. cit.*, p. 202.

Both movements defended the inspiration and infallibility of the Bible, but the Pietists stressed the inspiration
of the writers more than of the words. Spener accepted
verbal inspiration but not a mechanical dictation. Also in
Pietism there is a concept of continuing revelation. John
Robinson, seventeenth-century Puritan, avowed: "The
Lord has more truth and light yet to break forth out of
his holy Word." While the danger in Pietism is spiritualism, the danger in fundamentalism is scribalism.

Again the worship of the early Pietists and Puritans
was characterized by reverence and awe. Zinzendorf
emphasized the need for a "hushed silence" in approach-
ing the throne of God. Johann Franck in his celebrated
hymn "Deck Thyself, My Soul, with Gladness" spoke of
greeting Christ "with loving reverence" and "trembling
awe and wonder." In modern revivalism and fundamentalism the gulf between God and man is often obscured,
and an undue familiarity with God is encouraged. The
possession of Christ is stressed more than the adoration
of Christ in much fundamentalist revivalism, though here
it must be said that many theological conservatives of our
time, particularly those in the Reformed and Lutheran
traditions, also emphasize the need for a spirit of reverence and wonder in worship. An attitude of reverence
does not cancel out joyful spontaneity, but it does exclude flippancy and ecstatic abandon. It is the churches
of a dead orthodoxy and an arid liberalism, not those of
evangelical Pietism, that are generally characterized by an
enervating tedium and mournful solemnity.

We need also to recognize that the early Pietists had a
high view of the sacraments. Zinzendorf's piety was
marked by a lively fervor toward the Eucharist. Wesley
too is noted for his Eucharistic piety. The Pietists likewise made a place for such sacramental rites as confession
and confirmation, though mandatory confession was
frowned upon. The fundamentalists have been anti-sacra-
mental; the sacraments become ordinances of the church,
and the emphasis is placed on obedience to Christ's

commands rather than on mystical participation in Christ. Some dispensationalists even see no value in water-baptism.

Again the Pietists were mistrustful of the role of reason in preparing the way for faith while modern fundamentalism is remarkably open to philosophy and natural theology. Spener attacked the dependence of theology on the "heathen philosophy" of Aristotle; his criticisms were aimed at Protestant orthodoxy. Tersteegen declared: "Oh! Reason, be still! The sea is all too wide and all too deep; here is no soil for all thy wisdom and thy speculation."[57] While apologetics figures very highly in fundamentalism, the Pietists were much more concerned with sermons, diaries and devotional manuals. When Charles Spurgeon was asked if he would defend the Bible he replied: "I would as soon defend a lion." Whereas the fundamentalists have generally sought to make the faith credible to the modern mind, the Pietists were content simply to testify to and herald the faith. Tersteegen reflected this anti-apologetic stance in his words: "Conversion is the work of God's Spirit, and not the achievement of man's persuasion." The noted conservative evangelical D. Martyn Lloyd-Jones, former pastor of Westminster Chapel, London, is closer to original Puritanism than modern fundamentalism in the distinction that he draws between the religious and scientific approach to truth; while the latter is based on the knowledge that man can acquire by his reason and senses, the former is founded on divine revelation.[58]

The position of Jonathan Edwards is especially interesting, since he is the father of much of modern conservative evangelicalism in America. He wrote: "The gospel of the blessed God does not go abroad a-begging for its evidence . . . it has its highest and most proper evidence in

57 Nigg, *op. cit.*, p. 224.

58 D. Martyn Lloyd-Jones, *The Approach to Truth: Scientific and Religious* (London: Tyndale, 1967).

itself."[59]   Yet he believed that external arguments may
have some value. They may on occasion awaken (but not
convert) unbelievers, and they can confirm the faith of
believers. For the most part, Edwards maintained a reserved and even a negative attitude toward the apologetic
arguments for the faith. In his view,

> it is but very lately that these arguments have been set in a
> clear and convincing light, even by learned men themselves;
> and since it has been done, there never were fewer thorough
> believers among those who have been educated in the true
> religion. Infidelity never prevailed so much in any age as in
> this, wherein these arguments are handled to the greatest
> advantage.[60]

Both Pietism and fundamentalism see the necessity for
an experiential appropriation of the truth of faith. They
both are intent on doing justice to the subjective pole of
salvation. Yet while the fundamentalists speak of decisions for Christ and a crisis experience of conversion the
Pietists were more likely to lay emphasis on the struggle
toward repentance and bearing the cross. Samuel Rutherford, the Westminster divine, avowed: "Heaven is a strong
castle that has to be taken by force."[61]   And again:
"Remember that it is violent sweating and striving that
alone taketh heaven."[62]   Edwards held that "sudden conversions were very often false" and that "God never
bestows salvation until men seek it earnestly." The cheap
grace that is so prevalent in modern popular revivalism
was certainly not present in original Pietism. Francis
Schaeffer reflects his Puritan heritage when he contends
that one should never invite a person to accept Christ as
Savior without warning him to count the cost.

Both movements emphasize the grace of God as well as
the obligation of the believer to lead a Christian life.

---

[59] Jonathan Edwards, *Religious Affections*, p. 123.

[60] *Ibid.*

[61] Whyte, *op. cit.*, p. 116.

[62] *Ibid.*

Francke contended that it is through "the overwhelming greatness and power of the Lord" that the individual rises "from the natural state to the state of grace." The Pietists were insistent that union with God is achieved only through the grace of God and not the initiative of man. Nevertheless Pietism as well as fundamentalism has been imperiled by synergism; this is evident in the Pietist doctrine of the prepared heart, but the modern movement, because of its reliance on rational arguments and revivalistic techniques, is much more vulnerable to this charge. The peril of legalism also appeared in both movements, but this is inevitable when the commandments of God are given special emphasis. Zinzendorf warned against the temptation of legalism when he said: "It is not the moral man but the new man who counts."[63]

We do not wish to disparage the signal contributions of the fundamentalist movement. Men like Reuben A. Torrey, Arno C. Gaebelein and William B. Riley kept alive many of the evangelical concerns of the past, particularly the missionary mandate and the need for the new birth. Solid scholarship was evident in theologians like Benjamin Warfield and J. Gresham Machen. Machen in his book *Christianity and Liberalism* rightly perceived that there is an unbridgeable gulf between evangelical Christianity and liberalism as a system of thought, though he did not take adequate recognition of the fact that liberals can still be men of deep personal faith despite the errors in their thinking. For the most part the older conservatives called for schism, and perhaps they were right at the time. Yet we must not abandon the millions of evangelicals who still remain in the mainline churches, for they too need to be given a ministry. *Christianity Today* has estimated that 35 to 50 percent of the total constituency of the National Council of Churches are evangelical in their theological orientation, so we cannot simply write

---

[63] Arthur Mettler, "Count Zinzendorf" in *The Plough*, Vol. V, No. 3 (1957) [pp. 71-75], p. 75.

off a biblical renewal within these churches. And the tragic fact is that schism begets schism, as can be seen in the continued splintering of the fundamentalist movement.

Evangelicals should not spurn fellowship with those ecumenists and liberals who confess Jesus Christ as Lord and Savior. Liberalism as a theological system must of course be repudiated, but should not we seek reconciliation with liberals as persons? What we suggest is not a compromise with liberalism, which is out of the question, but a mutual reformation and conversion under the Word of God.

It is heartening to discern a new spirit of openness in the new breed of evangelicals, many of whom are the children of fundamentalism. In his complimentary review of Richard Coleman's *Issues of Theological Warfare: Evangelicals and Liberals* Clark Pinnock offers this note of reconciliation: "It is time we left behind the attitude 'I have all the answers, you have all the problems' and began to encounter one another with understanding and love in the spirit of the Gospel."[64] Such an attitude augurs well for the future of evangelicalism.

Strengths and Weaknesses

Among the weaknesses in Pietism might be mentioned the neglect of systematic theology and apologetics in favor of devotional and inspirational writings (*Erbauungsliteratur*). It has been said that the practical was emphasized to the detriment of the theoretical and intellectual. This is not wholly true, since the Pietists also produced doctors and scholars including Spener, Wesley, Edwards, Godet, Bengel, Edward Riggenbach and Kierkegaard. Spener, who spent the greater part of his ministry in the pastorate, nevertheless has been one of the most prolific writers in Lutheranism. He regularly corresponded with

[64] In *Christianity Today*, Vol. XVI, No. 24 (Sept. 15, 1972), p. 32.

the philosopher Leibniz on literary and historical problems. In addition he played a major role in the establishment of the University of Halle. August Francke was a professor of Oriental languages and then of theology at Halle.

At its best Pietism sought to hold in balance the practical and the theoretical, but especially in its later phases it tended to minimize intellectual accomplishment. It was not able to give an intellectual defense of the faith powerful enough to stem the tide toward naturalism and humanism. Some forms of latter-day Pietism even became suspicious of a confession of faith, contending that life is more important. But a refusal to spell out the foundational principles of faith may well mean the eventual dissolution of the faith. It should be noted that Pietists like Spener, Wesley, Edwards, Francke, Hauge and many others contended for doctrinal fidelity as well as personal piety.

Again there was in Pietism a too ready accommodation to the values and concerns of bourgeois culture, such as individualism, freedom and industry. This cultural accommodation was more marked in fundamentalism, where a virtual alliance was established, at least in some circles, with capitalism and nationalism. The new evangelicals today are seeking to disentangle the faith from this kind of cultural alliance.

In latter-day Pietism regeneration came to be interpreted as instant transformation, and the presence of sin in the Christian was thereby minimized. What afflicts the Christian, it was said, are faults, not sins. Those who emphasized the second blessing and entire sanctification were even more imperiled by a false security, though they were not wrong in their contention that there are new outpourings of the Spirit after conversion. This perfectionist error was not present in original Pietism and Puritanism. Samuel Rutherford could argue: "New washing, renewed application of purchased redemption, by that sacred blood that sealeth the free Covenant, is a thing of daily and hourly use to a poor sinner."[65]

The bent toward subjectivism can also be mentioned as a possible weakness in Pietism. The emphasis was on *fides qua creditur* (subjective faith) over *fides quae creditur* (objective faith). Barth accuses the Pietists of giving more attention to man's faith than to God's Word and thereby losing sight of the objective foundations of the faith. Salvation came to be seen as an interior change in the individual rather than the reconciling work of God in Jesus Christ. This stands in contrast to Calvin, for example, who said that we have in the death of Christ "the complete fulfillment of salvation" and that we "have been born anew" through the resurrection of Christ.[66]

At the same time we must bear in mind that there are two loci of salvation—the cross of Christ and the decision of faith. Salvation is not only a past accomplishment but a present experience. The Pietists emphasized the latter, but only because the church at that time was imperiled by a false objectivism. Ideally the Pietists sought to point men beyond themselves to the living Christ, but too often self-examination led to a preoccupation with self that denied the accomplished victory of Christ. Barth, in reacting against Pietism, maintained in his *Commentary on Romans* (1919) that the Holy Spirit "is our life-basis, not our experience." Forsyth too, in seeking to correct a misguided emphasis on subjective experience, declared: "Christ hides from us ourselves and our own subjectivity. There is a kind of piety which thinks more of self and its shortcomings than of Christ and his victory."[67]

To do justice to Pietism many of its guiding spirits were very much aware of the perils of subjectivism and

---

[65] Hugh Martin, ed., *Selected Letters of Samuel Rutherford* (London: SCM, 1957), p. 89.

[66] John Calvin, *Institutes of the Christian Religion*, II, 16, 13.

[67] Escott, *op. cit.*, p. 127.

sought to guard against it. Francke in his treatise *The Safe and Sacred Way of Faith* remarked: "As long as the heart finds nothing meritorious in itself, but everything in Christ, it moves in the realm of celestial bliss. . . . But when the heart no longer seeks salvation in the gracious forgiveness of sins through confidence in the merit of Christ, it is on the wrong track and finds no peace." In the view of both Spener and Francke dependence on oneself rather than on God is the way to damnation. Tersteegen, who was inclined toward mysticism, nevertheless asserted: "We must think more on God than on ourselves." For him contemplation of oneself only makes one ill. Carl Olaf Rosenius, writing in the nineteenth century, observed:

> These timorous souls make the mistake of gazing too long and too intently upon their sins and their evil propensities, even as the frivolous and thoughtless do not look upon them long enough for their own good. . . . Let them . . . look away from their sins and look to Christ, who has atoned for the sin of the world.[68]

The Pietists emphasized the life of the soul (*Seelenleben*), but they were not advocating a psychological analysis but a spiritual understanding of the soul seen in the light of the Word of God. The present-day encounter groups in which attention is focused on self-awareness and realizing one's own potential are a far cry from the prayer and discussion groups promoted by the early Pietists.

Sometimes in Pietism Christian brotherhood or community was seen as an ideal or goal that can be realized with sufficient faith. This notion was especially prevalent in the Age of Romanticism. Bonhoeffer voiced a criticism of this view: "Christian brotherhood is not an ideal which we must realize; it is rather a reality created by God in Christ in which we may participate."[69] And again: "Not

---

[68] Rosenius, *op. cit.*, p. 235.

[69] Dietrich Bonhoeffer, *Life Together* (N.Y.: Harper, 1954), p. 30.

what a man is in himself as a Christian, his spirituality and piety, constitutes the basis of our community; what determines our brotherhood is what that man is by reason of Christ."[70] At its best Pietism saw community as a fruit of mission.

The Pietists have also been criticized for placing too much trust in the rulers of the state, in the secular powers, to amend social ills. They tended to assume that social leadership was the exclusive business of the state. Here they were not so different from the modern secular theologians who pin their hopes for alleviating social ills on government action. In England and America Pietism in the form of Puritanism was characterized by a much greater political involvement.

Finally we must acknowledge that radical Pietism lost sight of the universal Lordship of Christ and tended to relegate the world entirely to the domain of Satan. In emphasizing redemption over creation it failed to do justice to the goodness of creation. Sometimes the impression was given that sanctification entails the denial of worldly goods and the suppression of one's humanity. Some of the Pietists would have difficulty in exulting with the Psalmist: "The earth is full of the steadfast love of the Lord" (Ps. 33:5). Little was said of the hidden Christ, who is present even among pagans (cf. Acts 17:26-28).

We cannot imitate the Pietists, nor should we seek a neo-Pietism. But we must not disavow their example. We agree with John Howard Yoder that in terms of the options open to them their response was creative and original.

The Pietists remind us that Christianity concerns life as well as doctrine, spiritual devotion as well as ethical action. They call to our attention that justification must continue in sanctification and be fulfilled in glorification. They also remind us that apart from striving after per-

70 *Ibid.*, p. 25.

sonal holiness no one will finally be received into the eternal kingdom of heaven (cf. Heb. 12:14). In the words of Frederic Godet, "the sincere quest of holiness is the living spring of the Christian life."

The Pietists stressed Christian practice, and this is just as important as Christian doctrine. Spener was noted for both *Fürsorge* (social work) and *Seelsorge* (the cure of souls). The same is true of many of the other leaders of Pietism. In Hebrews 13:15, 16 we read that the two necessary sacrifices are the praise of our lips and the sacrifice of our lives. For the Pietists word and deed go together. The mystical and the practical must be held together in creative tension. Yet Pietism is insistent that the highest kind of Christian practice is missions. Evangelism must always have priority, even though social service is its inevitable corollary.

If we were to list further signal contributions of the Pietist movement we might mention the following. First the notion that the fellowship of love is a genuine mark of the true church (with the Word and sacraments) was generally characteristic of Pietism, even if only implicitly; this view was especially pronounced in Zinzendorf's theology. The idea that evangelism in the sense of personal testimony is incumbent upon all Christians was also a special contribution of the Pietists. It is not sufficient to depend on the pastor and missionary; the believer himself must bear witness in his secular vocation to what Christ has done. This brings us to the priesthood of believers, which was given practical reality in the Pietist movement. Christians were encouraged to come together for prayer and mutual intercession, and here we see the spiritual priesthood in action. The view of the Pietists that preaching should be based on the Bible and animated by the Spirit was anticipated in some of the Catholic missionary orders and in the Protestant Reformation.

Again the Pietist contribution to hymnody must not be disregarded. A surprising number of the hymns of devotion in Protestant hymnals have come out of the

Pietist and evangelical awakenings. Zwingli had silenced all singing in worship. In many of the early Reformed churches the sung liturgy was restricted to the Psalter. The Pietists utilized popular folk tunes in bringing the gospel to the masses. Among the great hymn writers associated with German Pietism are Joachim Neander, Paul Gerhardt, Philip Nicolai, Johann Heermann, Tersteegen, Zinzendorf, Johann Schröder, Christian Keimann, Michael Schirmer, Johann Rambach, Benjamin Schmolck, Tobias Clausnitzer and Johann Franck. Though not all of these had an integral relation with the Pietist movement, their hymns reflected the spirit of Pietism and contributed to the flowering of evangelical devotion. In the English-speaking world we can mention William Cowper, Isaac Watts, Joseph Hart, John Bunyan, Augustus Toplady, William Williams, John Newton, Charles Wesley, Fanny Crosby and Robert Robinson. It should not be forgotten that both Luther and Calvin also wrote hymns; Luther's contribution is especially significant in evangelical Protestantism.

Finally the Pietists are noted for their emphasis on the role of spiritual counsel (*Seelsorge*) in the life of the church. Tersteegen, Spener, Baxter, Samuel Rutherford and many others became well known for their facility in the care and cure of souls. The conventicles themselves served as a means for spiritual guidance and nurture. Today this side of the Christian life has been taken over by pastoral psychology, but for the most part it seems to have been separated from its spiritual and theological roots.

Today the relevance of Pietism is becoming increasingly apparent. Even a secular commentator on society like Sidney Harris can write: "Violence is in the heart more than in the streets." What the Pietists were after was a new kind of man, and this sentiment is shared even by the radical Marxist, Herbert Marcuse. But the Pietists saw that this new kind of man must be a creation of God. The final answer to the social problem is the new birth.

The Pietists remind us that piety should not be sought as an end in itself. It is the by-product of something else—faith and surrender to Jesus Christ. It is also a means to the greater glory of God and the salvation of souls.

Index of Subjects

Index of Names